JUDSON PRESS
PUBLISHERS SINCE 1824

# Boomerangs to Arrows

»»»

## A Godly Guide for Launching Young Adult Children

**SHARON NORRIS ELLIOTT**

JUDSON PRESS
PUBLISHERS SINCE 1824

Boomerangs to Arrows: A Godly Guide for Launching Young Adult Children


Interior design by Beth Oberholtzer Design.
Cover design by Wendy Ronga, Hampton Design Group.

**Library of Congress Cataloging-in-Publication data**

Elliott, Sharon Norris, 1957–
Boomerangs to arrows : a godly guide for launching young adult children / Sharon Norris Elliott. — First edition
pages cm
ISBN 978-0-8170-1712-5 (pbk. : alk. paper) 1. Parent and adult child—Religious aspects—Christianity. 2. Adult children living with parents. 3. Adult children—Family relationships. 4. Adult children—Psychology. 5. Bible. Psalm CXXVII—Criticism, interpretation, etc. I. Title.
BV4529.E54 2013
248.8'45—dc23

2013004145

Printed in the U.S.A.
First Edition, 2013.

# Contents

# Introduction »»»

After speaking with frustrated parents of young adults about the topic of this book, at first I planned to entitle it "How to Get Your Grown Kids Out of Your House." Another title considered was "How Did You Do That?" referring to the question often asked of my husband and me when people hear that our boys had gone away to college and on into adult lives of their own. Trust me when I say the story is not quite as simple as that; so, not wishing to sound flippant, insensitive, or dishonest, I pretty quickly nixed those titles. The oldest son did come back for a few months, and the middle son is on his own, but has had a tough time of it financially. So far so good for the youngest, who has used both the opportunity of his birth position and his smarts to learn by watching the other two.

Still, although this when-to-cut-the-apron-strings topic isn't always the easiest to discuss, the conversation does come up, and when it does, the question and the aggravation persist. We love our children, but when they are no longer little kids, a new dynamic exists when all of us live under one roof. Most of us have no qualms about providing for our children as infants, toddlers, and school-age young'uns who were, by virtue of their age and skill set, unable to provide for themselves. But currently we're experiencing an undercurrent (or is that a tidal wave?) of discomfort because many of our households are harboring full-grown men and women—some with more education than we ever got—who expect to be treated as independent adults, but who are dependent upon our income for their basic food and shelter.

I realize young adults are still living at home with their parents for a variety of reasons, but whatever the reasons, the fact still remains that they are not on their own, and the questions arise: Should they be on their own? When will they be? Will they ever be? Can they make it? Are they ready?

Okay, so back to the drawing board I went, searching to find an appropriate slant and title for a book that would give both workable suggestions and an answer to the question that we were being asked. After praying about it, God spoke to my heart and said, "Do what you always do."

Genius, God, I thought (as the Lord's answers always are). What I do when I write is take my material straight from the Scriptures.

So I delved into the Bible for parenting information on this subject and found Psalm 127:5, which says, "Blessed is the [one] whose quiver is full of them [children]" (NIV, modified). A quiver holds arrows, yet thousands of young adults are returning home like boomerangs. Arrows are pointed and straight; boomerangs are bent.

The picture was clear. We parents are pronounced "happy" when we raise, aim, and launch arrows. Upon further investigation, I found the entirety of Psalm 127 to hold the key that we parents need to unlock the door holding the answer to our present dilemma. Walk with me through these truths, and let's discover how we can transform our boomerangs into arrows and launch our adult children into the adult lives that God means for them to live.

CHAPTER 1

# What about Arrows? »»»

"Mom. Dad. I'm home!"

Didn't those words ring as music to our ears when our children were seventeen years old and returned early, safe, and sound from an after-dark outing with friends? After tossing up that silent "thank you" prayer to God for keeping the bad guys away, we secretly gave ourselves a little credit too for raising such responsible young'uns. We may have even tucked this little memory away thinking, *This will be a fine testimony to share at couples' fellowship next week.*

After seven more years have passed, however, that "I'm home!" cry doesn't have the same effect anymore. Sure, we still love them, and we're still concerned for their welfare, but the part about raising such responsible young'uns—we're not feeling that quite so much. As twenty-four-year-olds, aren't they supposed to be out on their own, earning their own keep, living their own lives, making their own way?

"Boomerang kids" aren't a new phenomenan. This is a cyclical pattern brought about mainly by economic conditions. For example, during the Great Depression in the United States, many young adults lived with their parents. As the country recovered, the boomerang phenomenon began to recede. Whenever the economy peaks, kids move out; when it dips, kids move back home.

Article after article points to the fact that the overarching reason for this boomerang phenomenon is a financial one. Whether it's the recession, out-of-this-world housing costs, exorbitant student loans, a lost job, a financially devastating divorce, or out-of-control credit card debt, it's a money, money, money issue.

Numerous articles and opinions on this phenomenon lead to the conclusion that there is something that could have helped stave off this current crisis: teaching good financial habits to our children as they were growing up. This is possibly a current challenge because the parental generation may have had struggles with forming healthy financial habits as well. Later I'll delve more deeply into the discussion of what to do about it now, but if we're going to face the issue, we cannot place all of the blame on a floundering economy or irresponsible kids. Since the bad economy and job market are the first culprits being blamed, perhaps there are some initial evaluations we can make to head off the results that they can produce:

- What do we understand about the value of money and the principles of saving, tithing, and living within one's means?
- Did we foster an atmosphere of fiscal responsibility or of fiscal negligence as our children grew up? How did we do it?
- What age-appropriate chores and responsibilities were our children expected to handle? What views did we hold about paying children for completing their chores or responsibilities? Were there some jobs that we expected our children to complete simply as responsible members of the family?
- What is our definition of a positive work ethic, and how did we foster that thought in our children?
- How did we handle times when a child tried but failed at an assignment or at fulfilling a responsibility? How did we justify our response, whether we corrected the failure, congratulated the try, or rewarded the effort?
- If a chore, assignment, or activity proved to be a bit strenuous, how did we handle it if our children refused to participate?

- What kinds of excuses, if any, did we make for our children's behavior if others judged it in a negative way?
- What was our response if our children broke household rules?
- If in a remarriage, how did we handle it when the new step-parent needed to render correction? What was our response if adversarial conditions arose between our children and our new spouse?
- What percentage of our children's requests was fulfilled? In other words, did we give our kids virtually everything they asked for? If so, why? If not, why not?
- How did we feel and then react when our kids wanted the latest, greatest, and most fashionable items even when our budget and status didn't allow for those things?
- What part did we feel responsible for in assisting with our children's college expenses? Did we sufficiently evaluate whether we or they could actually afford the colleges they wished to attend?
- What is our definition of "adulthood"? Do we see adulthood as independence and detachment from parents, or do we see adulthood as something else?

Each generation over the past hundred years seems to have done better than its parents economically—each generation until now. In our affluence, we may have afflicted our children with "affluenza." Somehow kids seem to have caught the diseased notion that they get to start at the top. If they can't do that, they'd just as soon not start at all. In our well-meaning effort to protect them from the pains of poverty or struggle, perhaps we've hampered them from growing the muscles of intestinal fortitude. By shielding them from the heat of the sun called Lack, we've kept them from essential vitamins D and G—Determination and Grit.

I'll never forget a *Cosby Show* episode in which Vanessa told her friends the cost of an expensive painting that hung in the Huxtable home. Her friends took her information as braggadocio and labeled her "little rich girl," a label that offended her. When she related the incident to her parents, her father, Cliff Huxtable, said, "Let's understand one thing. Your mother and I are rich. You have nothing."

Cliff and Claire were teaching Vanessa a valuable lesson. Yes, the comforts of home were spilling over onto her, but the effort to earn those comforts wasn't hers. If those rich benefits were to continue once she was grown, she'd have to earn her own title.

According to a Pew Research analysis poll of Census Bureau data, "the share of Americans living in multi-generational family households is the highest it has been since the 1950s, having increased significantly in the past five years. Adults ages 25 to 34 are among the most likely to be living in multi-generational households: In 2010, 21.6 percent lived in this type of household, up from 15.8 percent in 2000 (the vast majority were living with their parents)."[1] And an article by Joe Plemon written in 2010 entitled "Boomerang Kids—How to Handle Them Returning to the Nest," the author says, "Nearly 1 in 7 [American] parents with grown children had a 'boomerang kid' move back home last year."[2]

Yes, the economy has been in a terrible slump. Yes, thousands of highly educated young adults are streaming out of universities, degrees in hand, and are flooding the already tight job market. Yes, young people are delaying marriage in record numbers, causing many of them to discover how hard it is to make it alone. Times are tough, so these young folks come home, and sometimes they do so with more than our permission. They actually return at our urging.

Is this the best possible arrangement or life move for our adult children? Should they expect to continue living with their parents, or should they have a vision for living independently? Adulthood and independence go together. Are we parents doing the best we can when it comes to building that understanding into our kids?

The difference in moving back home this time as opposed to previous generations is the overall attitude of entitlement that seems to be the undercurrent. Completely apart from a recessionary climate, what has contributed to the mentality of many young folks who take it for granted that even as full-grown adults they can have a key to a home, unlimited access to a fully stocked refrigerator, and an open door to request financial assistance without paying anything for those privileges?

Maybe we're sitting in the middle of a perfect storm. Consider these issues of our times:

- A college education opens doors, so we've strongly encouraged our high school graduates to continue their schooling.
- Rising costs on everything in our culture has led to thousands of college students borrowing hundreds of thousands of dollars to pay for their college degrees.
- Multitudes of highly educated college graduates are now propelled into an oversaturated job market.
- Parents have had to deal with the "rights of the child" governmental climate and the push of the media toward political correctness, permissive parenting, and tolerance of anything and everything.
- Considering all of the above, parents feel pressure to offer the open-door policy to young adults to move back home after college or to stay home after high school.
- The invitation to move back home is then misconstrued as an open-ended invitation to stay indefinitely without the obligations of contributing to basic living expenses or an expectation of a move-out date.

Consider two contemporary examples of young adults living at home with their parents: one from a television reality show, and one from a respected news show. In the reality show, the mother (hereafter referred to as "Mom") in the family took the opportunity to trade places with another person completely opposite in lifestyle and personality. The exchange person was appalled to move into the guest room of Mom's home only to find two very healthy twenty-something adult males (Mom's sons) still living at home. As Mom and Dad left the home daily to attend full-time jobs, these sons stayed home between their part-time college classes, enjoying a beautiful home, all the food they could eat, and all the water, gas, and electricity they could use. Mom and Dad even supplied cell phones that the boys used all throughout each day to contact their friends using social media. Did they help cook? No. Did they clean up? No. Did they do their own laundry? No. Were they thinking about moving out? No. Why should they?

Would you move out of a rent-free, utilities-free, $750,000 home with maid service? These boys were obviously healthy and intelligent, but they thought nothing at all of living off of their parents. One even voiced as much, saying, "Why should we move when we have everything we need right here? We couldn't afford to live like this on our own."

On the news show, the interviewer tried to remain objective as he reported on the following story. He was examining the boomerang phenomenon and interviewed a family in which there was a young, female, recent college graduate with a bachelor's degree in graphic design. This young woman worked very part-time waiting on tables, and her salary was a mere $65 a week. (The federal minimum wage is $7.25. At this rate, she was working only nine hours per week.) She would not search for a job anywhere else except for in her chosen field, so that she could use her talent. Her mother had taken an extra job to pay for the daughter's extra financial weight (more food, higher electric bill, etc.). The daughter even complained about how hard it was to get along with her parents as an adult because she felt treated like a child, with their demands for cleanliness around the house, and with a curfew.

The boomerang phenomenon is happening across the Pond in the United Kingdom as well. Paul Majendie writes, "Boomerang kids who treat the family home like a free hotel are driving their parents to distraction. . . . Government figures show that 58 percent of men and 39 percent of women aged 20–24 live with their parents in England. Weighed down with student debt, battling to get onto the housing ladder, marrying much later than their parents' generation, they find the family home is an easy and attractive option."[3]

Debt is nothing new; neither are aging, maturing, and responsibility. They all seem to go together naturally just as the expected move from childhood through adolescence and on to adulthood flows. In their study about youth and adolescence, Jeffrey Jensen Arnett and Susan Taber point out that "cultures characterized by broad socialization encourage independence, individualism, and self-expression."[4] Indeed, our current culture prizes independence, individualism, and self-expression. Arnett and Taber go on to discuss young people who grow up in such an environment:

> Most young people in such cultures may first consider themselves to be entering adulthood when they begin to establish residential and financial independence. This means relinquishing the role of dependent child and taking greater responsibility for themselves. . . . Thus, the crucial role of transition to adulthood in a culture characterized by broad socialization involves moving out of the role of dependent, subordinate child, and into the role of independent, self-sufficient member of society.[5]

If this is true, the enlightenment and self-expression of our culture means that young adults, regardless of financial pressures, should be flocking away from their parents' homes rather than back to them. Perhaps Newt Gingrich's interesting perspective may shed some light on the problem. He observes that prior to the nineteenth century, adolescence did not exist. He claims,

> Adolescence was invented in the 19th century to enable middle-class families to keep their children out of sweatshops. But it has degenerated into a process of enforced boredom and age segregation that has produced one of the most destructive social arrangements in human history: consigning 13-year-old males to learning from 15-year-old males.[6]

He further argues,

> The costs of this social experiment have been horrendous. For the poor who most need to make money, learn seriously, and accumulate resources, adolescence has helped crush their future. By trapping poor people in bad schools, with no work opportunities and no culture of responsibility, we have left them in poverty, in gangs, in drugs, and in irresponsible sexual activity. As a result, we have ruined several generations of poor people who might have made it if we had provided a different model of being young. And for too many

> middle-class and wealthier young Americans, adolescence has been an excuse to delay work, family, and achievement—and thus contribute less to their own well-being and that of their communities.[7]

Recent psychological findings at first seem to disagree with Mr. Gingrich and volley the ball back into the let-them-move-back-home court. A new understanding of maturity being bantered about claims that adolescence doesn't really end until age twenty-eight! Australian psychologist Dr. Darryl Cross states that late-ending adolescence "is related to earlier physical changes with the younger kids."[8] Dr. Cross goes on to explain that the social changes caused by young adults still living in the home negatively affect the maturation process of the younger kids.

Dr. Michael Carr-Gregg, a fellow professional of Dr. Cross, concurs with this observation, and he adds that parents need to set boundaries both earlier and later in their children's lives. "Parents at the moment are bad at setting and monitoring boundaries. . . . The truth is, when you've got a young child, you should be monitoring how often they're on the internet, what they're looking at. And if you've got an adult child in their 20s who you feel should be moving out, then sit down with them and discuss what they need to do. Too many just let it go."[9]

So, if an eighteen-year-old can vote, smoke, marry, give his or her life for the country, and be tried in a court of law as an adult, aren't we sending an incredibly mixed signal by taking other normal adult responsibilities—such as living on one's own, paying one's own bills, buying and preparing one's own food—off the table (a table that they ought to own as well)? Something's not adding up here.

Psychologists, politicians, journalists, educators, and parents can toss around theories all day long, and indeed I have given them some space here to do just that. But is there an answer to the question "What should we do with these big people still living at home?"

I believe there's always an answer if we start with a source that's always right. God's word has something to say about parenting adult children. Consider Psalm 127:

> [1]Unless the Lord builds the house, the builders labor in vain.
> Unless the LORD watches over the city, the guard stands watch in vain.
> [2]In vain you rise early and stay up late, toiling for food to eat—
> for he grants sleep to those he loves.
> [3]Children are a heritage from the LORD, offspring a reward from him.
> [4]Like arrows in the hands of a warrior are children born in one's youth.
> [5]Blessed is the [one] whose quiver is full of them.
> They will not be put to shame when they contend with their opponents in court. (NIV, modified)

Here at the start, particularly consider verses 3a and 5a: "Children are a heritage from the LORD. . . . Blessed is the [one] whose quiver is full of them." On the surface, these verses seem only to be making a case for having a big family. There's nothing wrong with big families, but there's so much more to these words.

God is comparing our children to arrows because that's what is carried around in a quiver. God chose to use this metaphor to teach us something, but I wondered what that something might be. So, I did the next logical thing: I embarked upon a little research about arrows.

An arrow is planed to ensure its smoothness and straightness. The shaft is sanded, cut, and coated. The cresting bands of color wound around the shaft identify the arrow's owner, and the arrow is said to be "fletched" when it is adorned with feathers. The shape of the arrowhead is determined by the purpose for which the arrow is used.

What does all of this mean for us? I contend that God compared children with arrows because, like arrows, children are supposed to be aimed toward a target, a purpose. As we extend this metaphor, parents then become the crafters, employed by the Master Archer, to sand, smooth, cut (not physically, mind you, but through thoughtful and prayerful educating and discipline), and coat each arrow-child. We watch closely for clues to determine God's design for our children—our arrows—that which God has already placed in the product. We parents are the archers, responsible as directed by God for aiming and adequately launching each arrow toward the target of independent adult lives.

Quivers are full of arrows, not boomerangs. Arrows fly straight and sure; boomerangs return. Nothing in Psalm 127 speaks of boomerangs.

Arrows are linear; boomerangs are bent. As they are growing up, we tell our children, "Stand up tall, hold your head up, look people directly in the eye, be proud and sure of yourself, be a woman, be a man." All of these phrases work alongside the definition of the word *straight*, but not of the word *bent*. An object that is straight "has the same direction throughout its length"; and when we say that someone is "being straight" with us, we mean that such a person is "upright and direct, honest, sincere, outspoken, not blended with anything or slanted." The word *straight* is listed as an antonym of the word *bent*. As we journey through the rest of this book and Psalm 127, may we solidify our mindset and the way we view our adult children, understanding that they are meant to leave home and live as independent adults.

»»» **PARENTAL PAUSE:** Let's go back and evaluate ourselves. Using these statements taken from the thoughts posed earlier in this chapter, survey your past parenting techniques by simply and honestly responding on a scale of 1 to 5, 5 being "handled excellently," and 1 being "never even thought about it."

| | |
|---|---|
| 1. I raised my children to understand the value of money and the principles of saving, tithing, and living within one's means. | 1 2 3 4 5 |
| 2. I fostered an atmosphere of fiscal responsibility. | 1 2 3 4 5 |
| 3. My child was given age-appropriate chores and responsibilities. | 1 2 3 4 5 |
| 4. I expected my child to complete, without pay, jobs that were his or her responsibility simply as a member of the family. | 1 2 3 4 5 |

| | |
|---|---|
| 5. I rewarded my child when he or she excelled. | 1 2 3 4 5 |
| 6. If a chore, assignment, or activity was a bit strenuous, I encouraged my child to stretch and grow through participation. | 1 2 3 4 5 |
| 7. My child suffered the consequences of his or her own mistakes without my making excuses for him or her. | 1 2 3 4 5 |
| 8. I enforced household rules, extending disciplinary repercussions when those rules were broken. | 1 2 3 4 5 |
| 9. [If applicable] When I remarried, I allowed my new spouse to render proper correction and loving discipline when necessary to my kids. | 1 2 3 4 5 |
| 10. I stayed within our family budget when my kids asked for things, even if that meant they had to go without the coveted luxury. | 1 2 3 4 5 |
| 11. I was adequately prepared to assist my child with his or her college expenses. | 1 2 3 4 5 |
| 12. I guided my child toward an educational institution he or she could afford. | 1 2 3 4 5 |
| 13. From a young age, I placed within my children the idea that adulthood meant independence, and independence meant detachment from me. | 1 2 3 4 5 |

Every circumstance is different, and in a later chapter I'll discuss those instances that could necessitate a boomerang stay. Exceptional circumstances would include adult children with clinical special needs; those needing protection from an abusive boyfriend, girlfriend, or spouse; or those going through the initial stage of a life change (divorce, desertion, home from the military, those just a few months out of college, or those who have experienced some sort of devastation). We also will look more closely at seasonal boomerang kids in a later chapter.

First though, since general guidelines and policies are best devised not upon exceptions or special cases but rather on revealed principle, let's delve a little more deeply into the basic premise and the heart of God on this matter of adult children living independently. When exceptions arise, we ought always look to move back to our scriptural and spiritual center as quickly as possible. So now, let's explore the relationship between the bow and the arrow.

**NOTES**

1. Pew Research Center analysis of U.S. Decennial Census data, 1940–2000 and 2010 American Community Survey (IPUMS), "Rising Share of Young Adults Living in Multi-Generational Households: Percentage of adults 25–34 living in a multi-generational household." (Statistic found in "The Boomerang Generation: Feeling OK about Living with Mom and Dad" by Kim Parker, March 15, 2012, as reported in Pew Research Social & Demographic Trends, www.PewSocialTrends.org.)

2. Joe Plemon, "Boomerang Kids—How to Handle Them Returning to the Nest," *Christian PF*, March 19, 2010, http://christianpf.com/boomerang-kids/ (accessed May 29, 2013).

3. Paul Majendie, "'Boomerang Kids' Driving Parents to Distraction," *Reuters Life!*, February 7, 2008, http://mobile.reuters.com/article/lifestyleMolt/idUSSAT75557420080207 (accessed May 29, 2013).

4. Jeffrey Jensen Arnett and Susan Taber, "Adolescence Terminable and Interminable: When Does Adolescence End?" *Journal of Youth and Adolescence* 23, no. 5 (1994): 517–37.

5. Ibid.

6. Newt Gingrich, "Let's End Adolescence," *Bloomberg Businessweek*, October 29, 2008, http://www.businessweek.com/stories/2008-10-29/newt-gingrich-lets-end-adolescence (accessed May 29, 2013).

7. Ibid.

8. Callie Watson, "Adolescence Doesn't End Until You're 28," *Adelaide Now*, April 2, 2010, http://www.adelaidenow.com.au/news/south-australia/adolescence-doesnt-end-until-youre-28/story-e6frea83-1225848748222 (accessed May 30, 2013).

9. Ibid.

## CHAPTER 2

# Bows and Arrows »»»

Unless the LORD builds the house, the builders labor in vain.

PSALM 127:1a

I may not know much about construction, but I do know that an architect is the one who designs the buildings. Without an initial vision, there would be no structure at all. The architect takes his or her vision and translates it into a plan, and then the builders follow that plan to erect the structure. If the building is to come out as envisioned, the construction workers need only to follow the plan. It is neither the job nor the prerogative of the workers to change the architect's plan.

God is the architect of the family. It was God's original idea and vision. The original family consisted of the husband and the wife, and then it expanded to include their children. God, the Master Builder, has given parents—the construction workers—the plan for building the character, esteem, and so forth of their children. Incorporating the metaphor laid out in Psalm 127:4, we see parents as the bow in the hands of the Master Warrior responsible for the carrying, aiming, and accurately sending forth their arrows—their children.

Scripture depicts the family early in the first book of the Bible. Genesis 2:23-24 states, "The man said, 'This *is* now bone of my bones and flesh of my flesh; she shall be called "woman," for she was taken out of man.' That is why a man leaves his father and mother and is united to his wife, and they become one flesh" (NIV).

After we read of the debacle of original sin in Genesis 3, the story of the first family is taken up in Genesis 4.

> Adam made love to his wife Eve, and she became pregnant and gave birth to Cain. She said, "With the help of the LORD I have brought forth a man." Later she gave birth to his brother Abel. Now Abel kept flocks, and Cain worked the soil. In the course of time Cain brought some of the fruits of the soil as an offering to the LORD. And Abel also brought an offering—fat portions from some of the firstborn of his flock. (Genesis 4:1-4a, NIV)

Notice the plan for the family that God lays out:

1. Adam had a "job" (a responsibility) before he had a wife (see Genesis 2:15).
2. Eve was specially made for Adam and was brought to him with her gifts and talents to help him accomplish their joint purpose.
3. Sexual relations and the bearing of children happened after Adam and Eve were joined as husband and wife—that is, after they became a family.
4. Their children, Cain and Abel, also had jobs (responsibilities) as adults.
5. The children followed in their parents' footsteps, serving the Lord.

## God's Original Blueprint for the Family

According to Psalm 127, the theme passage for this book, verse 1a says, "Unless the LORD builds the house, the builders labor in vain." If we are not about the business of building our families the way God planned for them to be built, we very well could be constructing on shifting sand, hoping that there will never be any liquefaction.

We start our families out on the right path if we begin with God's mindset about the family. Granted, none of us can go back and undo our situation if we got things out of order, but we at least need to start now acknowledging God's intent. The hard truth is that some of our issues with our boomerang children may hinge on the fact that we didn't do things right to begin with.

»»» **PARENTAL PAUSE:** Maybe your family was not built using God's original plan. Don't despair. God not only builds new families, but renovates old ones. Take time to speak with the Lord here about the renovations needed in your family structure.

- It may be time to start by confessing some structural damage that you brought upon your own building.
- Then it might be necessary to ask the Holy Spirit to help you shed your old beliefs about what family should be, and replace those old values with God's mindset about the family. You can't begin to build or renovate using blueprints that you don't understand or refuse to acknowledge.
- Finally, ask God to begin to show you how to take the first steps in your family's renovation process, especially regarding your grown children who are still living at home with you.

## Renovations Needed

All families will have troubles because all of us are sinful, imperfect beings doing our best to live out a sinless, perfect plan. Even when a nuclear family is doing its best to follow the biblical blueprint, conflicts can be expected. And we know that even when we strive to follow the biblical principles for our lives, we still must depend upon God's grace to sustain us in a broken and wounded world. It's easy to understand, then, how things can begin to go awry when God's blueprint hasn't been used. I'll speak more of stepfamily issues in the next chapter, but let's concentrate here on some common tensions of nuclear families and see how these tensions may be affecting, leading to, or even encouraging our boomerang-kid dilemma.

Normal childrearing friction exists immediately when any two people become a couple simply because of the differences in how the husband and the wife were raised in their own families of origin. Each one may think that his or her family's way of doing things was "right," rather than realizing it was merely "different." And so we engage in a sort of ongoing "right/wrong/different" debate.

The understanding of right, wrong, or different became a source of contention in my own household. Because of the strict rules that his mother enforced, my husband and his siblings all left home immediately after graduating from high school. Because all of them did it, he considers it "right" for all children to immediately leave home upon high school graduation.

My household upbringing was different. My brother left for the military right after high school, and my sister went to college and then to the military. But when I went to college, I commuted from home for two years before I spent my last two university years away from home in the dorm. Before I graduated, I had secured a full-time teaching position with benefits. I also owned my own car, paid my own car loan and insurance, financed my own phone, clothing, and social life, and had begun establishing my own credit. However, after receiving my bachelor's degree, I returned to live in my parents' home until I got married, five years later. There was no rules conflict, so I came and went as an adult, sharing a room in their home, paying my own bills, cooking some meals, and pitching in with chores.

The week after I married, however, before I even returned from my honeymoon, my parents had rented out my room to another boarder. I had not felt entitled to live there, nor had they allowed me to miss out on learning how to responsibly pay my own way.

My husband's siblings were eager to leave home, so they did. My siblings joined the military, which necessitated that they leave home, but my road from home took a bit longer. None of the above cases were "the right way to do things" or "the wrong way to do things"; they were simply individual cases handled differently. However, in both families, once we children became young adults, we were gainfully employed and did not impose financial or functional dependence upon our parents.

Leaving home or staying at home as a young adult is not a moral issue. Morality deals with the rightness or wrongness of an action. So, your eternal home in heaven or hell will not be determined by whether or not your young adult stays or leaves! But just as it's best for us to start a savings plan for the inevitable rainy day, so it seems to be an extremely good idea for young people to begin living as responsible adults early in those young-adult years.

Guidance from us as parents is the key to making this transitional time successful. Many parents are extremely nervous about letting their little birds fly from the nest. What if they fall in with the wrong crowd? What if my daughter gets pregnant, or what if my son gets a girl pregnant? How will they find their way around at a campus far from the familiar surroundings of our hometown? What happens if they don't know how to register for classes or don't get along with roommates? Or run out of money? Or wander into the wrong neighborhood? What will they do if they lose their keys, or have car trouble, or get into a car accident? What if they get in trouble with the police? What if they are assaulted or sexually molested?

Everything that we could ask can be thought through, and indeed should have been discussed anyway, before our children graduate from high school. After all, these concerns don't exist only when our kids leave home. It's a great idea to stress early the expectation and excitement that you feel about their leaving home and starting their own awesome, independent lives when they reach adulthood. In normal conversation, talk about what to do in case of emergencies, choosing the right kinds of friends, and sexual abstinence until marriage. Think of your direction of them in the context of what you believe God designed young adults to do—to mature and make the transition to independent adult living during their college years.

An additional positive reality of these "leave home" conversations is that they are as much about our kids as they are about us. Most of us must admit that it takes some preparation on our part to get ready for that inevitable day. If, as we all hope, we've experienced more encouraging than discouraging days while raising our children, seeing them leave the nest could be bittersweet. Not only do we love them, but also we know the perils and pitfalls that lay ahead for them in adulthood. There's no need to feel bad about the twinge of fear mixed with anxiety that runs through our veins when we consider letting go. The more we think and talk about the reality of the oncoming adulthood (because their adulthood will keep creeping up on them and us), the more we'll get comfortable with the idea of their independence.

The major complaints that I hear from parents concern young adults disrespecting their parents' homes, feeling entitled to be there, infringing upon their parents' retirement funds, and cramping their parents' retirement lifestyle by remaining dependent long after the college years. Consider the nightmare story I heard of a young woman in her mid-twenties who moved back into her mother's home espousing a list of rules by which her mom was supposed to abide. The unbelievable thing is that the mother is obeying the rules. When it's the mother's house, that's absolutely absurd!

The above story, though an extreme example, illustrates how some parents themselves are contributing to the boomerangism. Parents who encourage their children to stay home because of the parents' own misplaced needs are classic examples of folks living in codependency. For example, one single mom I interviewed while researching for this book kept her grown kids around to assuage her loneliness. Another received self-worth from her ongoing mothering role, even though she complained constantly about spending lots of her hard-earned income on her live-in, adult children's needs. Still another intentionally kept herself financially strapped to have an excuse to depend upon her children's incomes and thus keep them around. Strong, healthy, employed offspring should indeed support their aging and economically vulnerable parents, but in most cases it's not necessary to continue to live with them to do so.

## It's Me, It's Me, O Lord

An old gospel spiritual says, "It's me, it's me, O Lord, standing in the need of prayer." Before we lay too much blame on our kids for still being home, I'm a firm believer in pointing the finger back at ourselves. If we're not careful, our missteps can spill over into the psyches of our children. When they become young adults, our misguidance of them can come back with a fury, especially if they are still living under our same roof.

It might make you feel better to know that even biblical parents had a hand in screwing up the psyches of their children. Not only can we receive some empathy, but also, hopefully, we can receive some avoidance wisdom if we take a look at some of the Bible's faulty-parenting pointers.

### *Favoritism*

The preferential treatment that Isaac and Rebekah showered on their boys, Esau and Jacob, caused them to lose years of family harmony. Isaac loved Esau, his firstborn, because Esau was the outdoor, rugged, hunting type of guy—a man's man, some would say. Rebekah catered to Jacob because he was a deep thinker who enjoyed the quieter activities closer to home. These parents had received a clear prophecy that the older son (Esau) would serve the younger son (Jacob), which was a backward arrangement according to society's norm at the time. Still, Isaac's preference of Esau moved him to disregard what God had said and summon Esau to give him the blessing of the firstborn, which would have placed Esau in the ruling position over his brother. When Rebekah coaxed Jacob, her favorite, to deceive his father and steal his brother's blessing, the parents lost both adult sons on the same day. Jacob had to run for his life when his brother found out what he had done. Then Esau lost the respect that he had for his parents, and so to hurt them, he left home and married foreign women.

As our young adults launch into their adult lives, their departure can and should be a joyous separation rather than a rebellious, anxious, contentious, or defiant one.

Isaac and Rebekah's overt favoritism resulted in the same way favoritism always eventually does, in separation. If not remedied, favoritism will drive a wedge between the children and cause them as adults to separate from their parents and from each other. The sad outcome is this: people end up living out that which they have learned, even if those habits were negative. As much as the children hated being treated differently as they were growing up, the practice had been firmly established, and they probably will end up practicing favoritism between their own kids. Nowhere is this exact point more clearly seen than in the life of Jacob, Isaac and Rebekah's younger boy.

Unfortunately, Jacob perpetuated the favoritism trend by showing overt preferential treatment to one of his youngest sons. Joseph was the firstborn son of Jacob's favorite wife, Rachel. The problem was, Jacob had ten other sons before Joseph. Reuben, the eldest, should have received the blessing of the firstborn. If he died or was somehow otherwise disqualified, Simeon was next in line. The succession would then have passed to Levi and so on, but Jacob skipped over all ten of the older brothers to favor Joseph. Jacob showed his preference openly too by making for Joseph a coat of many colors. This coat publicly confirmed Jacob's intention that when he died, Joseph would rule over his brothers as the family patriarch. When Joseph started having dreams confirming this, the brothers had had enough. Genesis 37:18-20 reports,

> But they saw him in the distance, and before he reached them, they plotted to kill him. "Here comes that dreamer!" they said to each other. "Come now, let's kill him and throw him into one of these cisterns and say that a ferocious animal devoured him. Then we'll see what comes of his dreams." (NIV)

The favoritism that Jacob showed to Joseph deprived Jacob of his favorite son for many years when those other brothers sold Joseph into slavery.

### *Jealousy*

A different branch of this same extended family fostered another problem among the kids: jealousy. This was brought on by Laban,

Jacob's uncle (his mother's brother) and future father-in-law. Laban's underhanded scheming to achieve his own ends pitted his own daughters against each other.

Jacob met and fell in love with Rachel. He made a deal with Laban, her father, to work for him for seven years in order to marry her. At the end of those years, Laban secretly switched Rachel with her older sister, Leah, and Jacob ended up marrying Leah (who also was not the pretty one). Laban's shady explanation was that it wasn't the custom in their land that the younger marry before the older, so a new deal was struck—in Laban's favor, of course. If Jacob spent one week with Leah, he then could have Rachel, but with one little catch: he must work for Laban for seven more years. How scandalous!

Thanks to their father's devious, self-centered trickery, Leah and Rachel jealously competed with each other for their husband's affection well into their adult years. One problem was that neither girl truly left her conniving father's house even after they married Jacob, so Laban still held sway over them.

We parents foster jealousy between our kids when we use them in our schemes. Children can catch a vibe that makes them feel that they must compete with each other for their parents' recognition. Each of them wants to be the one who makes mom and dad happy by being the catalyst to get mom and dad what they want. We are hindering our children's maturing process when we keep them around—perhaps even keeping them at home—because of some kind of selfish ends of our own.

Of course, it sometimes is true that family jealousy is the child's issue and was not fostered by the parents. Take the case of the Hendrickson family (all the names I use here are not the real names). The scenario is all-too-familiar. Lesli was the baby sister, and although all five Hendrickson children were attended to well by their parents, the oldest sister, Cerise, felt slighted by the little sister everyone else adored. Cerise wasn't able to go to private school because when she was born, the parents were just squeaking by to put enough food on the table and have a roof over their heads. By the time Lesli came along, Mr. and Mrs. Hendrickson were much better off financially, so Lesli attended private school. The girls' personalities and activity choices differed as well. Cerise participated in art competitions, but Lesli was a cheerleader. Cerise won the local spelling bee, but Lesli was homecoming queen. Although Cerise had accomplishments, Lesli seemed to outshine everything Cerise could do. Mr. and Mrs. Hendrickson gave the same kinds of kudos to all the children, but Cerise held a particular, seething dislike of the little sister who was popular, talented, and, in the eyes of others, pretty much faultless.

In cases like this, parents need to be attentive to what's brewing in their children's hearts so that they can nip the jealousy demon in the bud. It's important to give each child his or her just due, but also it's vital to encourage each child to be proud of his or her siblings. For this point, it is helpful to take a clue from the apostle Paul's words concerning how members of the body of Christ ought to act toward one another. He said, "The members [of the body] should have the same care for one another. If one member suffers, all suffer together with it; if one member is honored, all rejoice together with it" (1 Corinthians 12:25-26, NRSV). We can raise our children to relate to their other siblings in the same way. If they are proud of each other's accomplishments, they will applaud successes rather than being jealous of them.

Reading about Isaac and Rebekah, Jacob and Esau, Leah and Rachel, and even Lesli and Cerise, we can understand how pervasive and insidious favoritism and jealousy can be in the lives of our young adult children. These problems only serve to aggravate an already explosive situation if those young adults have boomeranged back home or have never left in the first place.

#### »»» PARENTAL PAUSE:

- What are your expectations for your children's living arrangements once they graduate from high school?
- Can you speak with your spouse about negative issues concerning your children without your spouse becoming defensive?
- What tensions regarding your children have arisen that you have stifled and thus need to be openly and honestly discussed?

- Are you on the same page regarding your treatment of each of your children? Can you identify issues of favoritism and jealousy in your home? If so, begin to pray about how God would have you approach and root out these family destroyers.

### *Independence Sabotage*

Some parents are so wrapped up in their children that when the children are ready to leave, the parents no longer know what to do. These parents, seeing their kids becoming more and more independent, get scared, and so they begin to sabotage that independence.

Several families that I've heard of are suffering from reliance guilt and therefore participate in independence sabotage against their adult children. (The identifying statistics have been camouflaged here, so if this sounds like your family, it's definitely by coincidence.) For example, consider the situation in which a wife has lost her husband to death. After years of dependence upon him, she's frightened about her security and is unsure whether or not she has a purpose any longer. She knows one thing: her children love her and are concerned about her well-being now that she's alone. She wants them close. Her new habit is to lean heavily upon them to do things for her that she can readily do for herself. She also caters to the freeloading ones because they make her feel even more needed. Now a family rift is growing as the sponger adult children pressure the earning adult children to keep funneling resources home to "take care of momma." Mom doesn't really mind the stress because the difficulties are keeping everyone around her, and whether she realizes it or not, that's her ultimate goal. As soon as anyone suggests sitting everyone down for a much-needed meeting, mom feigns a medical emergency, and the meeting is postponed indefinitely until she is feeling "more up to it." Subconsciously or not, mom is surviving on the turmoil because she feels that anything is better than the painful loneliness that she fears would invade her life without it.

Most people who I know would bend over backward to assist their aging or ill parents. However, when that assistance is given not out of pure love, but mainly as a result of a parent's manipulation, the result in the adult child's heart will be bitterness.

**»»» PARENTAL PAUSE:** To what degree are you guilty of sabotaging your child's (children's) independence in an effort to keep them close to you? Consider the truth of this adage: "If you love something, set it free. If it comes back, it is yours. If it doesn't, it never was."

## Adopting God's Parenting Style

There's a reason why the Bible uses the images of "father" (e.g., Isaiah 63:16) and "mother" (e.g., Isaiah 66:13) to make God known to us. God is a perfect parent, and the way God does things for, to, and with us gives us a huge clue as to how we ought to parent our own children. If we plan to raise arrows instead of boomerangs, let's start as "bows" that will mimic God's parenting style, a style that involves autonomy, advancement, and admiration.

### *Autonomy*

Think again about how God parented those first children. After breathing life into Adam, God gave him the responsibilities of caring for the garden and subduing the earth. Then God gave him a wife as a helper suitable to share in the work, and God expected them to carry out their duties.

Look at that. God did not form Adam, breathe life into him, and then move him around like a puppet. God built into Adam, and then later into Eve, some autonomy, some independence. God's actions said, "I've made you, I've empowered you, and I've provided for you. I'll always be here with you, but I now expect you to take what I have given and go handle your business."

Since God's parenting style involves autonomy, this means after our new birth and after some time under close parental upbringing, God expects for us to "move out." In other words, we should be acting on what we have learned about being God's children. For example, we shouldn't have to pray a special prayer asking whether or not we should tell the truth, pay our fair share of taxes, or witness to a neighbor. There are things that we should know are right to do, so we simply do them. Sure, the Lord remains our heavenly parent, but God expects us to grow up.

If we let the Lord build our houses, it's incumbent upon us to parent our children to develop autonomy and ultimately move out and into independence as well. We remain their loving parents just as God remains ours; however, there should be things they know to do on their own by the time adulthood hits—things like holding down a respectable job, taking care of one's own personal needs, and ultimately living independently in one's own apartment or house.

God actually prepares both parents and our children for this inevitability from day one. Mothers, especially, take note. After that very first cry of a newborn, one of the next actions, the cutting of the umbilical cord, is a huge clue! This child is an autonomous being, made to eventually separate.

Think of all the ways young children naturally work out the autonomy that God has placed in them:

- The umbilical cord is cut.
- Even as infants, children quickly start doing things for themselves that we no longer need to do for them. They:
  —Turn their heads
  —Roll over
  —Hold their own bottle
  —Sit up
  —Crawl
  —Stand up
  —Walk
  —Become potty trained
  —Dress themselves
- The ever-popular phrase spoken by toddlers, "I can do it myself," which, apparently, no one has to teach them, is one of the first full sentences that little kids utter (besides, of course, the selfish, "No, mine!").

### *Advancement*

Throughout Scripture we see God the Father dealing with his children and advancing them as they progress through life. God puts more and more trust in them and thus needs to spend less and less time handholding. David was tutored by Samuel at first. As David matures, the Scriptures follow his exploits as he makes decisions (both good and bad) as a man on his own. David still loves his times with the Lord (to see that, read the psalms), but he's no longer dependent upon the prophet or his earthly parents to live his life and rule the kingdom.

There must come a time in our children's lives when they can do things for themselves, make their own decisions, follow God for themselves, and pursue their own dreams. They will never reach that place if we continue to do everything for them. We can start teaching them with little things.

For example, I watched as the mother of a perfectly healthy nine-year-old boy reached to open the pop-top of his soda can. She had also spread out his napkin, made and cut his sandwich (diagonally, of course), opened his bag of chips, and poured the chips onto the paper plate. All this while he just sat there at the table and watched. When he looked back and forth from the can to her, that's when she reached to open that for him too. That's one can that should still be closed and sitting on the table. I could only imagine in what other ways she catered to this boy and what that would look like when he was twenty-eight and still living in her house because he was never required to do anything for himself.

Then again, one of my friends is a registrar at a junior college. A man well over the age of forty approached the counter to register—with his mother. The mom shared that she was not in good health and was concerned about her son's ability to survive in the event of her death. She admitted that he had never lived away from home on his own, and she had basically supported his sedentary lifestyle. Now that the realization of her shortened days had hit her, she was forcing him toward some education that could possibly lead to gainful employment. I wonder if she has been cutting his sandwiches and opening his sodas all his life as well.

Sometime after age three but well before age forty, separations need to be established. You know your children, your neighborhood, and this society. The decisions as to how much responsibility to give and when to give it aren't etched in stone, but the point is for us to force ourselves to notice that our children indeed do grow up. If we put time into giving them more responsibilities as they age, backed by our confidence in them, they will take on the challenge of doing things for themselves. Catering to their path of least resistance will only produce dependent grown-ups.

If God intends for us to move spiritually from milk to meat, we can be assured that we are doing the right thing as we mentor our children to advance in their independence from milk to meat as well. As it is age-appropriate, we can give our children responsibilities. Then it's our job to teach that each new advancement is accompanied by a loss and a gain—what I call the *advancement principle*. For example, when a child learns to hold her own bottle, she loses the luxury of being held and fed but gains the freedom and responsibility of turning that bottle up if she wants to satisfy her hunger. When a child learns to walk, he loses the comfort of being carried around and gains the freedom of self-navigation and the responsibility of watching where he is going. And when a child goes to school outside of the home, she loses the security of mommy or daddy always being around and gains freedom to form her own identity and the responsibility of operating in the social graces necessary for group activities and personal protection.

You can tell by the above examples that the advancement principle starts pretty early in our children's lives. Be encouraged to keep it going. When my boys started elementary school, they had to wear uniforms. The school was very strict, right down to the navy blue socks that matched the navy blue pants. From the start, my guys learned it was their responsibility to care for their uniforms. As kindergarteners, they knew that when they got home from school, they were to pin their socks to their pants before tossing them into the colored-clothes hamper. The white shirts went into the white hamper. Then, at the end of the week, they loaded the washing machine with each load of clothes, unloaded the dryer, and put their uniforms away to be ready for the next week. When they were about in second grade (now tall enough to get their clothes out of the top-loading washing machine and alert enough to measure the detergent accurately), I turned the whole job over to them. When they went away to college, there was no need for them to have the how-to-do-laundry lesson. Not only did they know how to sort and complete the process, but also they understood the value of having their own clothes ready for when they would next need them.

The advancement principle can also be encouraged in the areas of kids getting themselves up in time for school, riding public transportation, and getting all their homework done without World War III breaking out. Sure, you will watch your children for signs of maturity, but you will also nurture that maturity along in small, consistent steps as they age.

In terms of being away from home for a while, form secure friendships with other families, perhaps from church or scouting, and share times at each other's homes. Once you are comfortable with the habits and principles held by the other family, allow the children to spend the day at each other's houses. This can progress to sleepovers. By middle school, children probably are ready to go away for a few days or a week to summer camp. Educational camps are also fun activities away from mom and dad but are structured enough so that the children really don't have much time to think about being homesick.

If we plan to launch adult kids into adult lives, they must be taught this advancement principle of moving from milk to meat. It is found in Scripture, you know. Hebrews 5:12-14 states,

> In fact, though by this time you ought to be teachers, you need someone to teach you the elementary truths of God's word all over again. You need milk, not solid food! Anyone who lives on milk, being still an infant, is not acquainted with the teaching about righteousness. But solid food is for the mature, who by constant use have trained themselves to distinguish good from evil. (NIV)

What works in the spiritual realm for Christian believers works in the natural world for young adults. Believers are expected to advance or grow in their faith, moving in their understanding from the "elementary truths of God's word" to "solid food" prescribed to assist in distinguishing good from evil. Young adults are expected to mature into independent individuals, advancing past the elementary position of dependence upon their parents and moving to "solid food," which is the ability to fend for themselves.

As seen in the advancement principle, the progression to independence involves severing the apron strings and taking on the responsibility of providing for one's own shelter, food, clothing, transportation, and all the other various and sundry bills and obligations that adulthood demands.

Proverbs 17:21 says, "To have a fool for a child brings grief; there is no joy for the parent of a godless fool" (NIV).

»»» **PARENTAL PAUSE:** Take a personal inventory. What are you doing for your live-in young adult that he or she is old enough to do for himself or herself? If you died tonight, in what ways is your young adult child unprepared to continue living successfully without you? Here are some ideas that could help move your boomerang toward more personal independence:

- Discuss your live-in child's finances. Help your young adult plan how to handle financial responsibilities within his or her means. This will require that he or she divulge the amount earned on the paycheck and the outstanding bills, such as car loan, car insurance, education loans, and credit card balances.
- Make a budget together that includes shared household expenses, such as utilities, phone, food, and cleaning supplies. The portion of the house that your young adult uses to live there should also be added percentage-wise as rent.
- Formulate a transition plan that will help your young adult move toward autonomy and advancement.

### *Admiration*

Finally, God's parenting style involves not only autonomy and advancement, but also admiration. God's nature makes it easy for us to honor our Creator. In order to be parents to our kids in the same way God is a parent to us, we also must be honorable. Yes, the fifth commandment instructs children by saying, "Honor your father and your mother, so that you may live long in the land the LORD your God is giving you" (Exodus 20:12, NIV), but we are laboring in vain at this parenting job if we are not living as people whom our kids can honor effortlessly and honestly.

In this commandment, God places the relationship between parent and child in order. Children who have a legitimate reason to disrespect their parents have a hard time with this commandment. If we are living honorably, our children's respect is genuine, and we can expect to face immeasurably fewer hassles from our young-adult children when it's time for them to move into their adult lives. I'm not letting disrespectful kids off the hook, but I am suggesting that we be honest about any part that we may have played in their dishonorable ways.

Here are some practical principles that will help us allow the Lord to build our homes in the area of being admirable and "honorable" parents. An honorable parent is:

| | |
|---|---|
| <u>H</u>onest: | Honorable parents tell their children the truth. |
| <u>O</u>bjective: | Honorable parents are careful to steer clear of favoritism. |
| <u>N</u>atural: | Honorable parents admit their own shortcomings and failings. |
| <u>O</u>n Guard: | Honorable parents must protect their children physically, emotionally, and spiritually. |
| <u>R</u>egenerated: | Honorable parents follow after God, living out the change that Christ has made in their lives. |
| <u>A</u>ccessible: | Honorable parents keep the lines of communication open between themselves and their children. |
| <u>B</u>ehaved: | Honorable parents live by the Golden Rule and are mindful of how they act in public so as never to be an embarrassment to God, themselves, or their children. |
| <u>L</u>oving: | Honorable parents exhibit the two characteristics of thoughtfulness and discretion. |
| <u>E</u>difying: | Honorable parents are their children's biggest cheerleaders. |

»»» **PARENTAL PAUSE:** Look back over the nine "honorable" parent principles at left. What areas would you identify as your strengths as a parent? In what areas do you need to improve? Go through the list turning each statement into a question and then answer it. For example, ask yourself, "Do I tell my children the truth?" and "Do I show favoritism?" and "Do I admit my shortcomings to my children?"

## It's a Generational Thing with God

God is all about the family. How do we know that? Not only do physical traits pass to us from our ancestors' DNA, but also God has designed the family as a channel through which divine blessings will flow from generation to generation. This all started with the Abrahamic covenant when God told the patriarch, "In you all the families of the earth shall be blessed" (Genesis 12:3, NRSV). In Genesis 26 God reiterates this covenant to Abraham's son Isaac, and then God reminds him of where his blessings are based by saying, "I will bless you and will increase the number of your descendants *for the sake of my servant Abraham*" (Genesis 26:24, NIV [italics added]). The blessing was repeated again in Genesis 28 to Isaac's son Jacob. See how the blessings are rolling from generation to generation!

Be aware, though, that a channel is a channel. If blessings can flow from generation to generation, so can cursing. When we read the Ten Commandments, we see how this works. Exodus 20:5-6 says, "You shall not bow down to [idols] or worship them; for I, the LORD your God, am a jealous God, punishing the children for the sin of the parents to the third and fourth generation of those who hate me, but showing love to a thousand generations of those who love me and keep my commandments" (Exodus 20:5-6, NIV).

So we see why having a healthy, spiritually attuned family is so important. God designed family as a conduit to bless us, but that same conduit can carry junk if we let it. Picture a river flowing through lush, mountain greenery. From time to time, the water cascades from one level to the next in a beautiful waterfall. Each level is a generation, spilling the goodness from the heights in the continuous flow. However, if we pollute that river, the harmful elements will accumulate and wash downstream. Let us not be the source of the pollution; instead, may God's "clear water" of blessings overflow from parent to child, down through the generations, and multiply as fresher and fresher wonders.

We can take encouragement in our God, for whom blessings are a generational thing. Our prayers, faithfulness, and life example before our children will not go unrewarded. "So let's not allow ourselves to get fatigued doing good," the apostle Paul urges us. "At the right time we will harvest a good crop if we don't give up, or quit" (Galatians 6:9, The Message). In other words, let's not pollute the channel. If we keep our conduit clean, the blessings can flow unhindered to the next generation.

## Chapter Recap

When we follow God's blueprint for building the family, we allow the Lord to build our house. God's intention is for parents to raise children to become independent adults. Our foibles and failures to construct our families according to God's way have played a huge role in our present dilemma of entitlement-minded, live-in, boomerang young adults. Renovations of our thinking, and thus of our families, are not beyond God's ability. The remedy is the adoption and implementation of God's parenting style, which involves autonomy, advancement, and admiration. When the Lord builds the house, we can be sure that we have not labored in vain to build ours, and the blessings that God bestows will flow from generation to generation.

CHAPTER 3

# Step Bows and Step Arrows »»»

Unless the LORD builds the house, the builders labor in vain.

PSALM 127:1a

If you think the nuclear family has issues, you ain't seen nothin' yet! When the original, believing, married father and mother are not the only ones raising the original children, we're bound to have thrown a huge wrench into the works of how God's blueprint for the family was designed. There's a bit of applicable truth to our present discussion in the adage "Too many cooks spoil the broth." Although it may take a village to raise a child, the right combination of villagers matters. When said village consists of several mothers and fathers all commanding the same level of authority, it's easy to see how everyone involved could be on edge.

## Stepfamily Snags

Kids are amazingly adept at pitting their moms and dads against each other to get what they want, so just think of what happens when there are three or four parents involved. Throw in the fact that several of those parents probably aren't so happy with each other, or may be downright antagonistic. Now add the advancing age and the ever-emerging sense of independence of young adult children, and flare-ups are ripe to explode. Cries fly through the air, such as, "You're not my father!" or "Why do we have to do things like *that* now?" and the ever-popular "Why did you have to marry my dad?"

Unfortunately, we hear these barbs spring from mouths of young adults who enter the stepfamily situation carrying resentment over their parents' divorce, or over the one parent's remarriage after the other parent's death. But we must remember that acidic words squirting from the mouth are often fed by underground springs of a river of hurt in the heart.

Shakespeare's play *Hamlet* is a classic example of a young adult dealing with this hurt-heart problem at its extreme. Most likely, the stepparents we're considering here are not guilty of actually murdering the original father or mother, but in the eyes of some young adults that's very much like what has happened in the remarriage of the custodial parent.

Hamlet was a young adult still living at home. He was grieved over his father's untimely death, confused about his mother's ability to shed her sorrow and remarry so quickly, angered when he discovered his uncle (the new stepfather and king) was the assassin, and determined to avenge his father's murder. The same type of grief, confusion, anger, and vindictiveness can exist in the hearts of our boomerang young adults, and when they are living under the same roof with the (in their eyes) offending stepparent, there's going to be trouble.

Snags spring not only from the children, however. Stepparents can also have issues, not the least of which is being lopsided about their involvement and influence expectations. Some insensitive and misplaced comments from the mouths of birth parents to their new spouses are phrases such as "Don't touch my child" or "Don't you dare let *that* man (or woman) tell my child what to do." On the one hand, remarried people expect the new spouse to invest money and time into their new stepchildren, but they are critical when children who are disobedient or disrespectful receive deserved chastisement from that stepparent. Let's get real: a stepparent who takes on the responsibility to clothe, house, feed, protect, educate, love, and be concerned about a stepchild feels justified, and rightly so, to properly discipline said child when necessary.

Other lopsided expectations can crop up unexpectedly as well. For example, in our blended family, my husband's side of the family operates differently from mine when it comes to the telephone. He and his children have always talked with each other on the phone almost every day, sometimes more than once a day. My side of the family is not like that. We rarely hold conversations with each other over the phone, choosing rather to e-mail or text each other, and then that's still not every day.

The old right/wrong/different (see chapter 2) monster raised its ugly head over this unspoken expectation because my husband equates frequent phone conversations with how much he and his kids love each other. Since my boys didn't call frequently once they left for college, he took offense and equated their lack of contact with lack of love and respect. The boys don't call me a lot either, but in our side of the family's way of looking at things, that's a healthy sign that they are doing well and are successfully operating as independent adults. Both my husband and I had preached independence to them, but in living that out when they moved away to college, they took on my understanding of independence by not calling all the time. To them, not calling constantly was a sign that they were living out what he had built into them.

Understanding that different is just different—not right or wrong—is very important. This calling-habit difference is just one example of the type of problem that can be easily ironed out when both sides learn to accept differences rather than be threatened by them. Actions driven by different styles are not done to intentionally hurt anyone.

With that said, it's also important to remember the sin nature with which we were born. Incidents such as divorce and remarriage can bring out the worst in our children. We cannot afford to be naïve. Our children are just as capable as anyone's of becoming one of those kids who is sly and conniving about his or her resentment of the new parent. And unfortunately, if not handled immediately and head-on, problems in this area only magnify as children reach the teen and college-age years.

Parents must wisely be on the lookout for manipulation. For example, when Johnny knows that he's the pawn between his divorced mom and dad, he will play on mom's sympathies when the new stepdad needs to lay down the law. And when Susie realizes that she's the apple of her daddy's eye, she will be determined not to lose him to the new wife. Just think of how those scenarios may play themselves out when Johnny and Susie are young adults still living at home.

»»» **PARENTAL PAUSE (Part 1):** Answer these questions individually, apart from your spouse.

- To what degree can you speak with your spouse about all the children in your lives without your spouse becoming defensive?
- How do your stepchildren try to manipulate the household and upset the peace?
- What feels unbalanced about your spouse's relationship with his or her kids and with your kids?
- What do you see that's good about your children? Your spouse's children?
- What do you see that's negative about your children? Your spouse's children?
- Do you feel respected by your spouse's children?

»»» **PARENTAL PAUSE (Part 2):** When both parents really want to work things out and smooth out some of these stepparenting issues—straightening out our lopsided expectations, taming the right/wrong/different monster, and getting on one accord with our spouse—start by having a rational conversation. Try the following activity with your spouse.

1. Enter your next parenting conversation with the agreement that the way your personal family did things is not the only way things can be done. In other words, make it a point to have an open mind to the possibility that there may be another way of doing things.
2. Say one positive thing about your spouse's child(ren).
3. Both of you write down one stepchild problem or one thing you expected when your family blended that is not happening the way you envisioned.

4. Exchange papers. Read your spouse's expectation and explain to him or her what you feel he or she is saying. Do not try to solve the issue yet. Just be sure you totally understand your spouse's position.
5. Once you both agree that you understand the position, explain why you do not do things that way. Perhaps it never crossed your mind, or maybe you don't assign the same significance to the issue. Have this conversation with a nonaccusatory and a nonjudgmental tone. Remember, the point of this exercise is to see things the other person's way.
6. Be sure to handle just one issue each evening. Both of you make a determination to see the issue from the other spouse's point of view. Agree to:
   a. Try things one way or the other;
   b. Come up with a totally alternate idea that will work for your new family; or
   c. Agree to disagree—to never bring it up again, hold it against each other, or discuss it with anyone else. With this option, you are both agreeing to drop the issue and not harbor ill feelings in your heart toward each other over your inability to win the other over to your point of view.

## Biblical Stepfamily Drama

Before we go much further, let's remember that stepfamily drama is nothing new. If we want to do case studies on families that blended about as well as oil and water, we need to look no further than the Bible. Please read each of the following four stories in the Bible in their entirety for yourself, but know that there's nothing new under the sun when it comes to stepfamily drama.

1. Abraham, Sarah, and Hagar created a parenting triangle and dealt with the treating-the-other-kid-better syndrome (Genesis 16–21).
2. Jacob had four wives (two of whom were jealous sisters) and at least thirteen children, all living in the same household. In this story, we read of favoritism and jealousy (Genesis 29–50). (Jacob had learned all about favoritism from his parents, Isaac and Rebekah, which was discussed in chapter 2.)
3. David and Bathsheba faced power struggles among their children (2 Samuel 11–24; 1 Kings 1).

4. Herod, Herodias, and her daughter dealt with the pressure for favors that a stepchild will sometimes try to exert upon the stepparent (Matthew 14:3-12; Mark 6:17-29).

## Baby-Momma and Baby-Daddy Drama

Remarried people with children from former marriages may also face "baby-momma drama." For example, the divorced mom may accuse her ex-husband of treating the new wife and her children better than he treats his own kids, and she can be jealous of the relationship that her kids are establishing with their new stepmother.

Men aren't off the hook either. "Baby-daddy drama" creeps in if a father shows insensitivity toward his new wife, suggesting that his past childrearing experience (with his ex-wife) had been perfect, his kids are perfect, and heaven forbid that he has the nerve to imply that his ex-wife was a better mother in some area. No point of criticism about his kids, no matter how legitimate, can be leveled by the new wife. It can be a tough balancing act to bring a new wife into the mix, and some remarried dads don't handle it very well. In an effort to skip confrontation about their new wife's needs, they won't accept personal analysis of their own time distribution, insisting that the wife is jealous of his kids when in fact he's not putting the needs of his marriage in proper perspective.

When all these distractions exist, it's no wonder that confusion in the childrearing of young adults takes place. We may not even realize that the distractions are forcing us to forget to focus on the marriage relationship first. Without a strong marriage, we're unable to supply the direction that our young adults need to be ready and able to sustain themselves in their own homes. It's a hard truth to face, but perhaps we're so busy marrying, divorcing, and remarrying—or involving ourselves in relationships leading to having children out of wedlock—that we are not properly focusing on the children whom these relationships produce. And now that those children are grown, here we are, discussing the problem of a generation of grown children not living independently.

Stepfamilies are complicated, but living and thriving in them is not impossible. We are able, with God's help, to keep our wits about us, avoid pettiness, put our spouses first and our children second, and be determined to honor God with every decision that we make in our new household. We're adults, so we must live with our heads out of the sand. Instead of just letting life twist our families around, let's take charge and consider some possible realities for why the situation with our adult children is what it is today:

- Could our decline in married, two-parent households be at all related to the fact that so many older offspring aren't leaving the nest? If so, we may at least begin to speak favorably about the family as God has designed it. Let the Lord build the house, and a myriad of problematic issues vanish.
- Could the cry of women over the scarcity of "husband material" have anything to do with how many of our young-adult men are still living at home with mommy? If so, we can start getting those young men out, allowing them the challenge of making it on their own. Let the Lord build the house, and young men who can care for themselves on their own will be ready to properly partner with their wives in caring for their children.
- Could some of the devastating divorce statistics be altered if disagreements over the living arrangements, habits, and problems of grown children living at home were taken out of the mix? If so, we can make a concerted effort to discuss our expectations for our young adults early and openly in our new marriages. Let the Lord build the house, and talk everyone through an understanding of God's design. Even in the case of remarriage, people dedicated to following God's blueprint for the family can experience lasting, happy homes. Ultimately, our young adults will then trust God as they move into letting God build their own homes.

My spouse, James, and I have both experienced previous marriages. Before James proposed to me, he conducted a conference call with his three grown children to tell them his plan. They voiced their main concern, which was their dad taking on my two middle-school-aged sons. Their problem was not a jealousy issue, but rather uneasiness about their dad's patience-quotient, since he hadn't had kids in his house for quite some time. Once he quieted their apprehension (because he already knew that my boys were disciplined, respectful, and loving), his children accepted Matthew and Mark as their little brothers. And my kids were excited about having their new 6-foot, 7-inch big brother, Jerod, and two big sisters, Lori and Buffy. We had become a family, and although not to the same extent, my boys suffered a great loss right along with Jerod and Lori when Buffy suddenly and unexpectedly went home to be with the Lord not a full year later.

We know the remarriage statistics, so James and I were well aware of the fact that we had to view ourselves—him and me—as a team and see the two of us as a family unit first. Then and only then could relationships with both the biological and the stepchildren fall in line. God's plan for the home, coupled with our personal, Spirit-led preferences, had to be clearly communicated between us as husband and wife. Once that's done, all children involved have no other choice but to get on that program. We didn't always get that right, but we're getting better and better at it. Believe it or not, parents, we're in charge, and we can give ourselves permission to not allow ourselves to be dictated to by the whims of the kids.

»»» **PARENTAL PAUSE:** Do a personal check.

- How can you move your marriage into first place?
- Are you speaking the truth in love (see Ephesians 4:15) when you have some observation to make about your spouse's children?
- Are you caring for your spouse as you would your own body (see Ephesians 5:28) when you are interacting with your own biological children?
- Are you practicing the principle of mutual submission (see Ephesians 5:21) with one another when it is necessary to make a decision related to your children?
- Do you hinder your spouse's enjoyment of the children by your attitude toward his or her parenting choices?

Without getting into the biblical specifics of when we can and when we shouldn't take a new spouse (that would require another book!), one thing is a reality: remarriage happens. When we find ourselves in this situation with previous children involved, we must be very careful to keep God's original blueprint in view. God will guide our new family, great redeemer that our Lord is, and cause something beautiful to grow. Most importantly, as our children approach adulthood in their new stepfamily, they can form or maintain a balanced, godly perspective on the family. The ultimate goal is for these young people to then carry a biblical perception of the family into the homes that they will develop.

CHAPTER 4

# Quivered Arrows »»»

Unless the LORD watches
over the city, the guard
stands watch in vain.

PSALM 127:1b

The developmental stages of a new product are often shrouded in secrecy. The plans are kept under lock and key, the prototypes are shut away from prying eyes, and the developers are sworn to silence. Everything about it is protected until the time is right for the big reveal. And the precautions are justified. The company producing a competing product might get its cutthroat hands on the design, steal the secrets, and get a jump on being first at manufacturing a similar creation. And what if an actual prototype got out? In 2010 a huge stink arose when an Apple® employee accidentally left a prototype of the newest model of the iPhone® at a bar, where someone picked it up and sold it for $5,000 to Gizmodo, a design and technology blog.[1]

Well, if everything about a new model product is that important to protect, no wonder it's our natural instinct that moves us to jealously guard the development of our children until they are fully ready to be revealed to the world, fully functioning as all they can do and be.

As we continue to apply Psalm 127 to our current discussion, verse 1b informs us of the importance of working beside the Lord to "watch over the city." The relevant Hebrew word here is *shamar*, meaning "to guard." This suggests that we parents are responsible to hedge about, protect, preserve, save, and make our children sure. We must be awake about, alert to, and on the lookout for problems that might launch our kids into the world underdeveloped and too soon. And we must be watchful so that no adversary will steal the power of the secrets placed within them before they're able to rise to their full potential. If either of those tragedies happens, all our years of guarding our kids will have been spent in vain.

But notice this too: a guard is no longer needed when the owner is personally on the lookout. We've done our best at our job of actively guarding our children during the years leading up to young adulthood. We've worked during those first eighteen years, and on through the college transitional next four, as twenty-four-hour watchers to allow for the safe, healthy, and purposeful growth and maturity of our children. We've tried to guard them sufficiently through those formative years, so they'll have all the inner resources that they'll need to go out into the world, away from our homes, and be ready to guard themselves as stable, independent individuals. It seems as though we should be ready to launch our children—our arrows—into those adult lives.

Since Psalm 127 refers to children as arrows and to the quiver as the place that holds the arrows, we can safely draw a metaphorical relationship seeing arrows as our children and quivers as our homes or parenting styles.

Before arrows are sent anywhere, the archer keeps them close and safe inside a quiver; in other words, they are quivered arrows. So what exactly is a quiver?

The Boy Scouts of America program for a merit badge in archery describes different kinds of quivers: "Quivers hold your arrows when you are shooting. The style of quiver you choose will depend on the type of archery you shoot." Of the four kinds of quivers discussed, belt quivers are the most convenient. They "attach to your belt and allow you to reach arrows easily. Styles include vertical, diagonal, hip pocket, and holster."[2]

As parent-guards turned archers, we have a critical job to do with our "arrows," both during their childhood and through the critical, transitional ages of eighteen to twenty-two. There are some protections that we can set in place to insure, under God's guidance and to the best of our ability, the readiness of our arrow-children as they are shot out into the world in which they must live. As you read through the following anti-boomerang techniques, remember that the ultimate goal is to so thoroughly prepare our children for independence that they will have no need to boomerang back home. And since it's never too late to grow in our understanding of and impact upon each other, these techniques can be set into motion whether you are reading this book pre- or post-boomerang. So let's learn to aim and let those arrows fly!

### Anti-Boomerang Technique #1: Guard against Sameness

Almost every family I've ever met in which there is more than one child says the same thing: "My kids are as different as night and day. By the way they act, you wouldn't even believe they are part of the same family."

This is definitely true of our family. Our daughter Lori and our son Matthew are introspective, deep thinkers, loyal to the end, and easily shattered because they are so feeling-oriented. Buffy (Janelle, who is now with the Lord) was the strong, get-it-done-or-get-out-of-the-way type. She held and asserted her opinion and didn't care what anybody thought about it. Although she could be hurt, she would mask it with a stiff upper lip so as not to ever let that weakness show again. Jerod is more the easy going type. He's solid in his job, likes things to go as planned, and doesn't really like to rock the boat. He'll have a great time, but he'll take care of business when he has to. And then there's Mark, our youngest and freest spirit. If there's a good time to be had, Mark is there. The ultimate charmer, Mark is grounded enough to be highly responsible; however, he will never miss an opportunity to savor all the gusto that life has to offer.

Our children can be case studies for the personality styles originally thought up by Hippocrates. Lori and Matthew are mainly the so-called perfect melancholy temperament, Janelle the classic powerful choleric, Jared the peaceful phlegmatic, and Mark the popular sanguine. Wouldn't it have been a shame if we had tried to squeeze each one of these unique individuals into one mold or, worse yet, into each other's molds?

With children born into the world having personalities this diverse, the "quiver" in which they were raised had to be adjustable enough to supply support for each of their individual styles, yet consistent enough to provide stability to all. Believe me, we didn't always get it right. And I haven't even mentioned how throwing our own temperamental quirks as parents into the mix made things exciting. However, filtering the move-away-from-home discussions through the sieve of understanding each child's personality is sure to make those talks much more edifying for the child and much less stressful for you.

God made each of our children distinctive just as the Lord has done with each of yours. The Bible backs up this notion of created individuality in the most celebrated Scripture verse about childrearing in the whole book: "Start children off on the way they should go, and even when they are old they will not turn from it (Proverbs 22:6, NIV). To "the way they should go" the Amplified Bible adds "and in keeping with [the child's] individual gift or bent."

You see, through this proverb God is teaching us that each of our children was given to us individually predisposed to exhibit unique character traits and to ultimately carry out God's plan in their own unique way. Your free-spirited, talkative little girl may never be comfortable in a business suit behind a desk at a corporate law firm, as you wanted, but she may love the hectic schedule and ever-changing atmosphere of a mission field hospital. Your brooding young son might not be the most popular kid at school who gets voted as class president, as you were, but his meticulous attention to detail could make him perfect for the many technical jobs now in demand in our computer-dependent society.

The discussion here does not warrant space to launch into a full study of the personalities, but take my word for it, looking into this discipline will be well worth your time. I'm grateful that I found books about the personalities before I birthed my first son. Upon observation of my children and practice of the principles, my parenting skills blossomed, and so did my kids. God helped me appreciate the differences in my children and recognize each one's "bent." This helped me to guide, encourage, and even discipline them in ways most effective for each individual child. Then, as they grew, they could begin matching their own strengths with interests and occupations that best fit their own character traits. Consequently, a smooth path was paved as I saw them move from high school to college and on into occupations as independent adults away from our home. The separation, although it snuck up on me way too rapidly, turned out to be quite a natural occurrence.

I don't want to leave you with the impression that I'm a heartless mom who, when my kids went away to college, simply dusted off my hands and shouted, "They're finally gone! Now I can have my life, my house, my car, and my bathroom back." Not at all. In fact, although the separation was relatively smooth, I had my moments.

When Matthew went away to college, the transition was pretty easy for several reasons. First, although he lived on campus, he was at Biola University, a Christian college only about forty minutes away from our home. The second reason for the smooth transition with Matthew was the fact that Mark would still be at home for two more years. The nest may have been quieter, but it wasn't yet empty. So, after registration and all the hard work of shuttling Matthew's things from the cars into his dorm room, Matthew walked us back to my Toyota Highlander. We repositioned the back seat to transform the car back into a passenger vehicle, kissed and hugged goodbye, and he walked away. There weren't even any tears.

I actually expected much the same scene when it was time to drop Mark off at college. After all, I'd been through this before, and I'd spent all their lives preparing them for the moment, so Mark's departure should be no sweat. Not exactly what happened.

Mark chose to go to college halfway across the country. He would be attending Southern University in Baton Rouge, Louisiana—quite a "fer piece" from California. On parent weekend, when his dad and I arrived to register him, Mark got off the plane and started sneezing. His allergies and asthma kicked in, triggered by something in the Southern air. Quite concerned, my first thought was, *Where's the health center?*

After two long days of registration glitches and figuring out how to take care of all the business from thousands of miles away once we left, we finally got everything squared away. While his dad took the short flight from Louisiana to Texas to spend a few days with his sister, I was tasked with getting myself to the airport, returning the rental car, and coming home alone.

Once Mark was sufficiently settled in, it was time for me to leave. Mark had already made friends, so I drove him to the gymnasium on my way off campus. I pictured the perfect movie scene about to play out. I'd pull up outside the gym and park; he'd reach over from the passenger side and we'd hug goodbye. We'd look at each other just long enough to see a little tear form, make a joke, and then he'd jump out of the car. I'd start the engine and glance out of the window to see Mark standing there waving as I pulled off. I'd watch him through the rearview mirror as he dribbled the basketball up the walkway to the gym door. He'd turn to wave one more time. Again, not exactly what happened.

I drove him up to the gym and parked, all right. He also leaned over for a goodbye hug and got out of the car too, as I had expected. I turned the key in the ignition, and the car started. Then I looked out the window, but my right hand only made it a few inches from the steering wheel in preparation for the final wave. Mark was gone. No little tear, no joke, no final wave. I didn't even see the gym door swinging on its hinges.

So much for movie endings made with eighteen-year-old college freshmen. That sanguine personality took college by the horns and never turned back. I missed him terribly once I returned to the now truly empty nest. At first, I called several times a week, just to hear his voice and know that he was okay. I'd never been without my kids for any substantial length of time since the day they were born. It wasn't until he came home for Christmas and then left again that I had gotten used to the fact that he could survive without my daily hand in his affairs. Trusting him to God's hands allowed me to let him go.

No matter what age your child is, it's never too late to gain a better understanding of him or her. Give it a try. Gain some additional knowledge of your boomerang's personality type. I believe that this can serve as a major boon in your ability to help your child to move on into adult life.

The most comprehensive book that I've found on the topic is *Personality Plus for Parents*, by Florence Littauer. The author does an amazing job using proven principles that help you identify and comprehend your child's personality. The book even includes profiles and questionnaires, quick reference charts, and guidelines to help you understand how each parent/child personality combination interacts.

### »»» PARENTAL PAUSE:

- How is each one of your children uniquely different from his or her siblings?
- How is each one of your children like you? How is each one different?
- To what extent do you expect your children to be like you?
- What can you do to avoid squeezing each one of your children into a one-size-fits-all mold?
- What does each child want out of life?
- How do you celebrate the successes of your children?
- How do you rebuild your children's self-esteem when they have experienced failure?
- When have you heard yourself say, "Why can't you be more like your brother/sister?" To avoid the mistake of pitting one child against another, what can you say to your child instead of asking that question?

## Anti-Boomerang Technique #2: Guard against Sluggishness

Proverbs 6:6-9, in The Message version, is prefaced with the title "A Lesson from the Ant." It reads,

> You lazy fool, look at an ant. Watch it closely; let it teach you a thing or two. Nobody has to tell it what to do. All summer it stores up food; at harvest it stockpiles provisions. So how long are you going to laze around doing nothing? How long before you get out of bed? A nap here, a nap there, a day off here, a day off there, sit back, take it easy—do you know what comes next? Just this: You can look forward to a dirt-poor life, poverty your permanent houseguest!

Although these words were written many centuries years ago, do they sound familiar? Perhaps they sound like something your parents used to say to you. Even scarier, perhaps you heard your parents' voices emanating from your mouth as you said such words just yesterday to your own teens and young adults. However, sometimes a wide gap exists between preaching these words and teaching them practically.

Obviously, we see that these sentiments are much more than nagging or ranting. These words are true. Our kids truly can take a lesson from the lowly ant. Even an ant has enough sense in its microscopic brain to know that if it doesn't work, it won't survive. Industry means its continued existence.

This admonition against sluggishness is a vitally important lesson that is our responsibility to teach our children. We must guard against sloth, apathy, and listlessness. Somehow, some way, we must teach our children how to be responsible, how not to be lazy, how to get up and do what must be done, not only for themselves, but also for the benefit of the entire family.

When I sent out e-mails to call for personal stories concerning this area, one response echoed many others I heard, proving to me the need for some help on this point. Chaundra wrote,

> Clearly, I will need to buy and read the book to see how others have accomplished the task of getting their teens to consistently do chores to benefit the entire family, because I haven't. We have tried positive

> rewards such as allowance and negative reactions such as limited TV time or earlier bedtime—all to no avail. I look forward to getting a copy of your book!

If you are fighting against laziness with your young adult boomerang kid, this struggle probably didn't just start yesterday. Chaundra is dealing with teens under the age of eighteen, not yet legally able to be out of the house. If she doesn't get a handle on it now, she could very well face twenty-something boomerangs not willing to pitch in at all, but ready to assert the power of their size to get their way.

So exactly how do we guard against sluggishness or laziness? We can start by recognizing at least the following four truths about our children. (And the earlier we start this, the better.)

### *The World Does Not Revolve around Our Child*

Everything else in my world took a back seat to my new baby the moment he was born. I transformed into SuperMommy! I was completely overwhelmed with the reality that I was personally responsible for the life of another human being. My body had brought him forth, and now my body was readied to nourish him along. I searched the Scriptures, read books, watched TV shows, tuned into Christian radio. I was determined to use everything at my disposal to raise this kid well. I even lost a friend by failing to participate in or even acknowledge her wedding as it came just weeks after Matthew's birth.

Perhaps if I had simply looked out of the hospital window right after Matthew was born, I would have realized that I was the only one on the planet so totally wrapped up in him.

It's tough to look at ourselves in the mirror and see a helicopter parent staring back, but if we see him or her, we need to snap out of it. Thankfully, I grew out of that initial bewitching spell. Be aware though, that the temptation to stay wrapped up in our kids—seeing them as the only worthy children on earth and ourselves as their only salvation—is strong and always lurking in the wings, ready to pounce. Some parents never get over it, or they don't get over it until major (but still not irreparable) damage is done.

For our own good and for the good of our children, we simply must face the fact that the world does not revolve around them. Children come to us as selfish little individuals who, left to their own devices, will remain so. We don't help the situation by giving in to their every whim.

Children who grow up to believe that the world revolves around them become young adults oblivious to the fact that they must submit to others who could hold their destiny. These may include the young man who drops classes in college because he doesn't like the way the professor is teaching or because he doesn't understand why the term paper has to be written in a prescribed way. Or this is a person like a young lady I used to teach. After she graduated from high school, and I heard she was still living at home, I asked her mom how and what she was doing now. Her mom replied, "Oh, she's fine. It's just so hard to hold a job in this economy." That wasn't completely true. I subsequently discovered that the young lady was unemployed because she refused to remove her tongue ring, which was a violation of the dress code for her would-be employer.

Or how about the healthy nineteen-year-old who told his divorced mother, "I don't want to work," when she confronted him about how he was spending his time since high school graduation. You see, this fellow had made it through the twelfth grade on a wing and a prayer grade-wise, but he had been encouraged by his dad and coaches to keep playing basketball because that would be his ticket to a college scholarship and then playing professionally in the NBA (National Basketball Association). Even though no Division 1 school (or a D-2 or D-3 school, for that matter) was interested in recruiting him, the stars linger in his eyes. He's thinking that his play at the junior college will still garner him a million-dollar spot, and therefore, in his mind, he has no time to work. That boy is now living with his father, and, as far as I know, he's still unemployed and dreaming.

It's all fun and games to let our children pretend to be princes or princesses while visiting Disneyland®, but please, let's allow the fantasy stop there. The world is not at our child's beck and call, and so we shouldn't be either. Remember that as parents, we are our children's introduction to the world. Since we love them, we can bring them into reality slowly, but we must be sure to get them there. Young adults are better prepared to handle life independently if they come to realize early on that being part of a family and a civilized society means participating in the work required to keep those institutions going. This realization is the only one sure to produce young adults who will not be lazy when it's time to work and care for themselves.

Building a positive work ethic early is solid preparation for when the time does actually come to leave home. From 2 Thessalonians 3:10 we learn that the apostle Paul was still trying to teach this to adults when he said, "For even when we were with you, we gave you this rule: 'The one who is unwilling to work shall not eat'" (NIV). Young adults who have internalized a work ethic in the home understand this principle of responsibility and are less likely to boomerang back home once they leave.

Several moms shared with me their experiences in this area of helping their children overcome laziness and participate responsibly for the good of the entire family. Here are a couple of examples:

> For the last four years, a family chore is doing the school lunches. I have my three girls help me set up food for the week and make sure they have nutritious items in the lunches. The girls are also given a chore list, and we rotate the list every six months between the children so that everyone does all jobs at one time or another. I feel that the most important one is that they make lunches for each other. It gives them the responsibility to make sure that their sisters are well equipped with a good lunch. Let me tell you, on the occasions when the chore has been done incorrectly, they have heard about it from their sisters. That's much better than Mom telling them. —Laura

> Sometimes a child taking on increased responsibility becomes a necessity. When I had major surgery, I was unable to do normal household tasks for weeks. My husband commuted over an hour each way and worked twelve-hour days already, so my mother took care

of cooking, bringing us delicious hot suppers. But who would take care of the laundry and cleaning?

I had a talk with my husband about our two teenage boys, and how it was time for them to step up and help out consistently. We assigned our younger son, Joey (almost fifteen), the task of doing the family's laundry—whites, darks, and towels. Our older son, Ben (almost eighteen), would collect and empty the household trash and recycling daily and make sure that it was curbside on collection day. Other jobs, such as taking care of the dog, cleaning their rooms, and putting away clean dishes from the dishwasher, were divided between both boys.

I had taught Joey how to do laundry the summer before, so he remembered how to sort it by color. To help him remember the specifics, I put sticky notes on top of the dryer with instructions on water temperatures. Joey has now been doing the entire family's laundry for two months, and he never complains. It has become part of his routine. He stays after school for weightlifting with his football team, and then he comes home and throws laundry in the washing machine before doing his homework. When it's dry, he folds it and puts piles of clean clothes on each person's bed. On weekends he often does four to five loads of laundry from start to finish.

In this case, my boys have been willing to take on extra responsibility because they have seen me suffer through a long, painful recovery and realized that I could not physically handle many of the chores. I wish I had asked them to do more around the house prior to this, but I believe that the experience has taught them to appreciate the time and work that it takes to run a household. As an added bonus, I believe they have more compassion for their mom! —Beth

»»» **PARENTAL PAUSE:** Readers of this book are at different stages of parenting. No matter where you are in the process, it's never too early or too late to start helping your child develop a strong work ethic. In addition to instituting Laura's and Beth's ideas, here are some additional ways to teach your child that he or she is not the center of the universe:

- Put your infant on a feeding schedule. For example, a very young baby may need to nurse about every two to three hours for the first few weeks. If the baby is fussy at an hour and a half, play together, talk to him or her, change the diaper, but you control the feeding schedule. As children get older, continue to regulate meal times. This not only will keep you from running back and forth to the kitchen constantly, but also will promote healthier eating habits and reduce the probability of such problems as obesity and cavities.

- Teach your children manners, from basics such as "Please" and "Thank you" to saying "Excuse me" when they want to interrupt your conversation with someone. Encourage them to observe and wait patiently for an appropriate time to break in. If manners were required in the younger years, put your foot down gently yet firmly and communicate to your young adults that you expect mannerly respect now as well. Start by demonstrating those manners and showing that respect for them. Then simply refuse to respond to their conversation when posed to you in disrespectful tones.
- Have older children help with meal preparation, even being totally responsible for dinner from time to time. Why should it be that if mom or dad doesn't cook, nobody eats? Once children see what it takes to prepare a meal for the entire family, they will tend to be more appreciative and patient when all they have to do is sit down at the table and assuage their hunger.
- In the case of a boomerang living at home, make out a schedule of who prepares family meals. If the boomerang refuses to help, make it clear that you will not be cooking for him, nor will the food in the refrigerator that you buy be available to him. If he will not share in the work, he will not share in the provisions. Lock the refrigerator and cupboards if necessary.
- Assign your boomerang child the amount of household work and expenses that she would have if living outside of your home. If her room takes up one-eighth of the house, then one-eighth of the water, gas, trash, and light bills is her responsibility as well. No payment means no light bulbs, no privacy (take the door off of the room), and so on. Get creative with your insistence that your boomerang begin to carry her own weight.

### *Our Child Is Not Better Than Everyone Else's Child*

We guard against sluggishness or laziness when we realize that our child is not better than everyone else's child. I know it's tough. All of us are proud of our kids, and we love to revel in their accomplishments and their general cuteness. We're supposed to give them confidence and build their self-esteem. But trouble happens when our children's self-esteem is on steroids and/or when it depends upon the destruction of another child's.

A child who gets the idea of being better than others is tempted to feel entitled to service or special favors from them. This attitude fosters laziness. A child's mind thinks, "I'm the best, so the teacher (coach, team, employer) owes me." A child with a superiority complex tends toward laziness. The apostle Paul, in Romans 12:3-5, warns, "For by the grace given me I say to every one of you: Do not think of yourself more highly than you ought, but rather think of yourself with sober judgment, in accordance with the faith God has distributed to each of you. For just as each of us has one body with many members, and these members do not all have the same function, so in Christ we, though many, form one body, and each member belongs to all the others" (NIV).

So how do we help our children to have a balanced self-image? How do we pump them up and keep them humble at the same time? It's easier than you might think. First, just tell them the truth. Second, help them see the good in others.

Our son Mark was a natural athlete and exhibited physical prowess almost from the time he took his first steps. He could accurately handle any kind of ball from a very early age, but basketball was his passion.

I remember watching his first YMCA league game when he was five years old. He progressed amazingly—after that first game, in which he tossed the ball to the other team when they all came after him. Through the years, when he would make outstanding plays, I yelled from many a rock-hard gymnasium bleacher seat, "That's my kid!" Upon his high school graduation, he was awarded "Athlete of the Era."

Regardless of all that, no matter how many NBA hopes Mark fostered, I had to communicate to him one day that he needed to have a plan B. "You're squashing my dreams," he would counter. "You're five feet, nine inches tall," I responded. "More than likely, a spot on an NBA team is just not in your future." It was my job to help him face the cold, hard facts, so I did the math. There are thirty NBA teams, with about thirteen players on each team. That means there are approximately 390 players in the whole world on NBA team rosters. Then I estimated the number of all the guys on high school basketball teams just in the United States and realized that every one of those young men coveted one of those 390-or-so spots. Further, I noted that not every spot is open every year. Add to this the fact that players come from all over the world, and a rational young man—even an above-average player—should soon be able to realize that his realistic chances are slim to none. You can work the numbers with top-level professional football, hockey, baseball, and soccer, with pretty much the same results.

Mark took my advice, got good grades, and won acceptance into a fine university. Still, he pursued his dream and tried to walk on to his college team. The coach gave him no love at all. He hung around the gym anyway, helping the team, even practicing with them when he could.

His diligence worked in his favor in an unexpected way. He caught the eye of the women's basketball coach, who noticed his love for the game, understanding of the basics, and excellent work ethic. She took him on as a manager of the girls' team, affording him the privilege of traveling with them during his junior and senior years. He even garnered a championship ring for being a part of the organization when the women came out on top of their league one season.

It was neither easy nor fun to tell Mark that the odds were against his dream, but parenting has never been all about ease or enjoyment. Parenting is about training and truth, and sometimes we have to communicate the hard truths in order for our kids to move on. So what if our kid is not the best in the world at sports, art, sewing, math, science, or speech; she or he can do something, probably many things, well. We can be the parent who sees the truth, communicates that truth, and still be the wind beneath our child's wings.

In addition to telling our children the truth about their strengths and weaknesses, it's important to help them appreciate the strengths and gifts of others. We need one another in this life; no one is meant to make it alone. Some things that help kids understand this is participation in team sports, youth group, choir, band, or drama club. Letting our kids hear us compliment someone else's child from time to time is also good for them. It's also nice to allow our kids to overhear our adult conversations as we compliment everybody's children, not just our own.

Young adults with a balanced self-image and an appreciation of others' gifts avoid laziness because they understand their place on the team and their responsibility to pitch in. This understanding is part of a great foundation on which to stand as they launch into adult life.

Even boomerangs can be encouraged to become part of a team. Although probably putting up a strong, possibly defiant front, they are not blind. They realize that other young people their age are landing good jobs, living on their own, and enjoying independent lives. If the job market is tight, encourage them to use their time beneficially and get involved with some sort of interest group. Maybe your daughter would like to join the softball team at the local park or a bowling league. Perhaps your son can volunteer at the Boys' Club or work with the teens at church. Community civic groups and political campaigns are also always looking for young volunteers. And a side benefit of volunteering with organizations such as the Urban League, Red Cross, World Vision, the local Democratic or Republican state office, and the NAACP is that your boomerang will rub shoulders with older, often well-connected people who could lead to, or offer a recommendation for, a permanent job because of that association.

### *Our Child Can Function apart from Us*

Our children have a better chance to grow up and not be lazy if we allow them to do things without us. Children are amazingly more capable of doing things without us than we might think. We just have to let them.

Mary Flett, a high school counselor and government teacher, tells of deciding to take her seniors on a field trip to the county courthouse. The school's budget was tight, so in searching for a means of transportation, she discovered that the Metrolink train ran directly past the building to which they were going. However, when she announced to the class that they'd be taking the train, she was surprised by how many of them were wary because they had never taken public transportation anywhere.

*No time like the present to add to our trip a new life lesson in city street survival*, Mary thought. The students learned how to read the train maps and schedules and figured out how to purchase tokens. They were a bit nervous on that first trip as they negotiated jumping on and off the trains in the crowds, finding seats, holding on, and watching for their correct stops. However, the next time they took a Metrolink train trip and added the lower grades to the journey, those seniors acted like seasoned urban commuters, guiding the rest of the students through the train-riding maze and experience.

It is built into kids to want to do things themselves, so let them do so within reason. Parents are still there to offer moral support and encouragement, to set rules and safety guidelines. Just as our children grow physically little by little, we can allow them to grow apart from us proportionately. If they separate from us little by little, it won't be such an enormous shock after high school or college graduation when they are actually packing those bags to move away from home.

When our boomerang is showing signs of superglue attachment, it's time to administer the solvent. As quiet as it's kept by the young-adult years, if the separation hasn't taken place already, we're attached to them just as much as they are attached to us. However, if you're reading this book, you're ready to be the one to instigate the severance. Start refusing to do things for your boomerang that you've seen other young adults of the same age do for themselves. If your child refuses to step up to the challenge, saying, "Okay, then, I just won't (do this or that)," you say, "Fine with me." Then go to the other room, turn on your favorite television show, and sit down to enjoy it. It won't be long before your boomerang gets the hint that you are serious. He or she will start finding a way from other sources (hopefully, eventually becoming independent) to do things without your assistance.

### *Our Child Needs to Contribute to the Good of Society*

Finally, in our discussion of guarding against sluggishness, we do so by teaching our young people the necessity of contributing some of their time, talent, and effort for the general good of society.

When I taught Charles Dickens's *A Christmas Carol* to high school students, I would point the students' attention toward the major themes of the novel. As we read about the rich miser, Ebenezer Scrooge, and his unwillingness to share his wealth even as he saw others suffering, we'd discuss one of those themes, which was the notion that everyone in society shares the responsibility to help the poor and uneducated. I allowed my students to banter that idea about. They'd inevitably debate questions such as these:

- Why don't the poor and uneducated just get up off their lazy duffs and take care of themselves?
- Why is it my responsibility to care for those outside of my family?
- If the rich (and who sets those standards) refuse to assist the poor and uneducated, should the government be involved in forcing the rich to give a certain portion of their wealth to charity?
- If I have more than enough for myself, why shouldn't I help?

These are poignant questions still facing humankind (thus the reason we keep reading classic literature over and over again), and cultures go round and round trying to answer them. Again, I submit that the Bible holds the definitive answer, a word that is apropos concerning our current discussion. For if we can prove that it is indeed everyone's responsibility to help the poor and uneducated, then we can pass along this truth to our young adults. Internalization of this reality will cause them to spend some of their valuable time in gainful employment, rather than waste away hours in idleness.

»»» **PARENTAL PAUSE:** Start a discussion with your young adults regarding their personal views about their responsibility to help society. Take note as to whether or not they have a heart for others or if most of what they say is all about themselves. You may even want to use some of the questions on the previous page with which my students grappled. The goal of this conversation is to emphasize looking beyond oneself for purpose and a reason to live. The ultimate objective here is to move your young adults to see that their independence will and should help them help others. Here are some Scripture verses to help guide your talk:

- Ecclesiastes 5:13: "I have seen a grievous evil under the sun: wealth hoarded to the harm of its owners" (NIV).
- 1 Timothy 6:17-19: "Command those who are rich in this present world not to be arrogant nor to put their hope in wealth, which is so uncertain, but to put their hope in God, who richly provides us with everything for our enjoyment. Command them to do good, to be rich in good deeds, and to be generous and willing to share. In this way they will lay up treasure for themselves as a firm foundation for the coming age, so that they may take hold of the life that is truly life" (NIV).
- Proverbs 11:24-25: "One person gives freely, yet gains even more; another withholds unduly, but comes to poverty. A generous person will prosper; whoever refreshes others will be refreshed" (NIV).
- Isaiah 32:8: "Generous people plan to do what is generous, and they stand firm in their generosity" (NLT).
- Hebrews 13:16: "And do not forget to do good and to share with others, for with such sacrifices God is pleased" (NIV).
- 1 John 3:17: "If anyone has material possessions and sees a brother or sister in need but has no pity on them, how can the love of God be in that person?" (NIV).

## Anti-Boomerang Technique #3: Guard against Excessive Self-Indulgence

Have you ever noticed how freely our young adults will spend our money, but how stingy they can be with spending their own? On the opposite end of the spectrum from guarding against sluggishness is the need to guard against excessive self-indulgence. Proverbs 30:8-9 says, "Keep falsehood and lies far from me; give me neither poverty nor riches, but give me only my daily bread. Otherwise, I may have too much and disown you and say, 'Who is the LORD?' Or I may become poor and steal, and so dishonor the name of my God" (NIV). Without our guidance and some lessons in balance, an employed young adult is apt to become either a miser or a spendthrift. The miser will want to stay home because she doesn't want to spend her own money, and the spendthrift will remain because he wants to spend it on nothing but pleasure. Both extremes—keeping it all just to watch it amass, and spending it all on enjoyment—are problematic and can turn an arrow into a boomerang.

Annette is your classic spendthrift. After graduating from a prestigious college, she moved back home from the dorm and was immediately employed in her field. Although she knew that payback of her student loan would start in six months, she operated in a sort of "out of sight, out of mind" manner. Her new paycheck seemed so large to her that instead of saving a bit of those first earnings to hedge against when that monthly bill would start rolling in, she figured she'd have no problem meeting that obligation once it started. Living with her parents, without the constant responsibility of rent and a food bill, she opened new credit card accounts and enjoyed new clothes and outings with her friends.

In six months time, almost her entire paycheck was going toward her credit debt, with the rest paying for gas for her car and personal care items. Needless to say, when those student loan payments started, her check barely stretched that far. It was now virtually impossible to move out because there was no money in her budget for rent and food. And God forbid that something would happen to the car.

On the other side of the scale we find Ashton. He too moved back home after graduation from a well-known university and secured employment working in his field. When the paychecks started rolling in, he opened a new savings account and started socking money away. He also immediately allowed the job to take money from each check for an IRA, life insurance, and profit sharing. Ashton left himself only enough cash each month for gas and a few lunches (he brown-bagged it most days, using the bread, tuna, and lunch meat that his mom purchased). He too had student loans to start paying back, and when that obligation came due, he simply saved less and made those payments.

So what's so bad about Ashton's situation, you may ask? He's a miser. Although he's watching his money grow, he's missing the point of being an independent adult man. First Timothy 6:10 speaks directly to his problem: "For the love of money is a root of all kinds of evil. Some people, eager for money, have wandered from the faith and pierced themselves with many griefs" (NIV). Miserly behavior is symptomatic of the "love of money" in several ways. For example, Ashton has made money his god; he idolizes it. In this, he has broken one of the first Commandments. By not helping to meet his own personal needs and depending on his mother's support unnecessarily, he is not honoring her, so another Commandment bites the dust.

Or what about Kathleen's daughter, Christine, who moved back home with her dad at the age of forty-five because of the downturn in the economy? After being back home with dad for two years, she's uncomfortable with her lifestyle with him. She doesn't really like her single dad's lifestyle, as the house is filled with cigarette smoke, alcohol, dad's friends, and his live-in girlfriend. However, Christine can't move out. Why? Dad has been financing her life for the past two years. Even with a master's degree in her field, the job market is so tight that she's still underemployed. Besides that, she has lacked the grounding that would have moved her to save and plan during the past two years of excess. For example, Dad provided the money for a job-hunting trip out of the country without a back-up plan. That same money could have been more wisely invested in the business venture she now wants to start.

Annette, Ashton, and Christine are participating in over self-indulgence. Annette is doing it by spending every dime, not saving or planning, and ending up with a full-time job yet no financial breathing room and completely ruined credit. Ashton is doing it by overlooking the admonitions to share one's blessings (1 Timothy 6:17-19) and give to the Lord (Luke 6:38). Christine is doing it by accepting dad's money for pleasure rather than for long-range planning to move into independence.

If it hasn't happened by high school graduation, we parents need to take on the role of financial educator and give our young adults a crash course in responsible money management. Make it a lesson, sit down with them, and show them your household expenses. A very graphic illustration would be to actually cash your paycheck, spread your bills out across the dining room table, and divvy up the cash on top of each bill. Your young adults will be amazed at how much money is laid before them and at how quickly it's swallowed up by the bills.

Follow this illustration with a discussion about responsibility and independence. Be sure to note the fact that their existence costs you money. For example, they're eating groceries; using water, gas, and electricity; and taking up square footage of the home for which you are paying. It is an anti-boomerang technique to give both misers and spendthrifts the awareness that there's a price tag on independence, and that price is paid by the adults who enjoy it.

**NOTES**

1. Eloise Harper, "Dude, Where's My Top Secret Next-Generation iPhone?" *ABC News*, April 21, 2010, http://abcnews.go.com/Technology/apple-engineer-gray-powell-lost-iphone/story?id=10430224 (accessed May 31, 2013).

2. Boy Scouts of America, *Merit Badge Series: Archery* (Brainerd, MN: Bang Printing, for the Boys Scouts of America, 2004), 21.

CHAPTER 5

# Sanded Arrows »»»

In vain you
rise up early.

PSALM 127:2a

Most parents I know discipline their children in one way or another; however, not all parental discipline seems to be effective to bring about the desired results. Why is that? I believe it is because not all discipline is connected with the correct ultimate goal, to raise children to become balanced, respectful, well-adjusted, God-honoring adults who are then able to do the same for the next generation. Discipline that is not connected to the ultimate goal is like rising early in vain. We're awake and ready, but nothing is being accomplished. The outward behavior of the child may be abated for the moment, but the inner attitude toward the transgression is the same. Let me give you another example of this concept.

Do you remember subordinate clauses from high school English? If not, let me refresh your memory. A subordinate or dependent clause is a group of words containing a subject and verb, but it can't stand alone as a complete thought. For example, the words "although Ingrid's grades dropped" is a subordinate clause because "grades" is the subject and "dropped" is the verb, but the complete meaning of that group of words doesn't exist until they are joined by an independent or main clause. We could add, "she still passed the class," and end up with the complete idea that says, "Although Ingrid's grades dropped, she still passed the class."

I use this example to show that although we may be doing something that seems complete to us, the major piece is really missing as it comes across to others. In regards to discipline, we feel like we're doing all the right things to keep our kids in line, but the rationale for it all is completely lost on our children. We're raising our voices, pointing our fingers, and getting high blood pressure in vain, all because the connection is not being made as to the whys of the rules.

As many of us became parents and raised kids, we probably just did what came naturally in regard to discipline. The kids disobeyed; we punished them. In many cases, we punished them the way we were punished. We doled out spankings or time-outs or restrictions or lectures, or some frustrated combination of all of these. We did whatever got those kids to stop the offending behavior. However, our disciplinary strategy often was like a subordinate clause if the major piece—including God in the disciplinary reasoning—was not intentionally joined to make our plan complete.

Thus the connection here with Psalm 127:2a, which says, "In vain you rise up early." The context of this verse refers back to the subordinate clause that begins verse 1: "Unless the LORD builds the house." You see, unless we realize that God is ultimately in control, all the early disciplinary work that we do with our kids could turn out to have been for naught. We are losing sleep over issues that we ought to have trusted to the Lord, following God's wisdom in regard to how to deal with our kids in that area.

It's amazing how much better we rest when we rely on God, the ultimate Watcher over every aspect of our lives, including how we raise our kids. When God is in control early on, we'll know what to look for and to correct about our kids' behavior. But do not despair. If you're reading this book with boomerang kids at home whom you want to have shove off, it's never too late to hit the "fast forward" button on these ideas.

»»» **PARENTAL PAUSE:** Quickly, right off the top of your head, name one positive thing and one negative thing that you have always noticed in your child, even from a young age.

## The Early Watch

An old adage says, "The early bird catches the worm." That means if we get an early start—a jump on something—we're likely to reap the benefit of whatever there is to be had. This principle applies in many areas of life. For example, from time to time a new technology is introduced into the market. When the iPad® was first introduced, news reports showed hundreds of eager customers lined up outside every Apple® store, wrapped around street corners and weaving through malls for hours or even days in advance. In another exemplary scenario, my own family joined other early birds every December 31. Our tradition was to camp out on Colorado Boulevard in Pasadena, California, in eager anticipation of having one of the prime spots to view the Rose Parade on the morning on January 1.

However much we may like being first to have the latest technology in hand or scoring front-row seats at parades, our effective early discipline of our kids is even more important. What we don't understand about how we deal with them can be crucial. We'd miss securing the new item if we stood in the wrong line, and we'd have spent a cold night outside for naught if we were on the wrong street. It's also vain to apply early discipline—rise up early—if we are not being watchful of the right things. And failure to watch in the right way makes us unsuccessful in our childrearing, ultimately leaving us with children who then fail to grow up, leave home, and enter the adult lives upon which they should embark.

So, if we do not wish for our watchfulness to be in vain, what kinds of things should we start as early as possible? Now, don't tune out: be of good cheer. Although it's best to look into the following areas early, hope is not lost if you are just coming into this knowledge with adult boomerangs in your second or third (or second *and* third) bedrooms. A pastor friend of mine used to say, "When you find more light, walk in it."

## Disciplining Tendencies

Some of my favorite movies are the Disney® films. A great line in *Jungle Book* applies to our current discussion. As Baloo the bear takes Mowgli the little orphan boy back to the human village, they meet all kinds of jungle residents and must learn their ways. When Mowgli comes across the elephant troop marching back and forth, he doesn't quite understand the motive of the continual drills. Colonel Hathi, the elephant leader, says, "Discipline: that's the thing!" You see, although no attack had ever reached that part of the jungle, and no credible danger had ever befallen the elephant band, Hathi understood the importance of discipline—just in case.

We should know enough about the world and about life's dangers that could befall our children to echo Colonel Hathi's proclamation. Say it with me: "Discipline: that's the thing!" The problem we face is this: since every child is different, how do we know exactly what areas to focus on with each child?

Well, there are some common areas in which every child should be disciplined. For instance, every child should know basic manners. Be polite, say "please" and "thank you," answer kindly when spoken to, and so on. When it comes to social etiquette, children should know that it's impolite to interrupt a conversation without saying "excuse me" or waiting for a natural break in the conversation. And they should learn to chew with their mouths closed, keep their elbows off the table, and let older people and parents with young children have their seat on a bus or in a crowded public place.

Additionally, though, each child was born with his or her individually peculiar tendencies. It's our job as parents to discover these tendencies, nip the negative ones in the bud, and encourage the positive ones to blossom. The encouragement side of this equation may come easily because we're generally watchful for those things in our kids about which we can brag. However, it may be a tad more difficult for us to pinpoint and then admit that our kids have issues—that is, negative tendencies with which they were born. These tendencies, if not corralled and brought under control, can easily lead to our children's prolonged immaturity and thus to a longer stay in our home. (The negative tendencies are also usually high-definition pictures of our own shortfalls, making them even more difficult to admit that we see.)

Our youngest son, Mark, has been a charmer from his earliest days. I realized the charming part in his first few weeks of life. He cooed and smiled instead of crying and screaming when he was hungry, sleepy, or discontent. Then, still in his infant stage, I began to notice how he'd cuddle close to any of my female friends wearing bright lipstick. As they held him, he'd stare up into their faces with the same smiles and coos he'd give me. My friends ate it up, and Mark was encouraged to cuddle all the more.

His charming ways didn't stop as he grew. He cajoled the first-grade teacher into believing that he could read much better than he could because he would eye-twinkle his way out of the more difficult assignments. In middle school, his height was right at the bust line of my high school students whom he always managed to approach with, "Can I get a hug?" I'd inevitably have to tell the girls, "Let him go."

This boy was destined to grow up to be a world-class player if I didn't do something about it. He'd likely want to be living off the women he could charm and con. It became my job early to train Mark about how to view, treat, respect, and care for women. They were not his playthings. I also needed to impress upon him that when the time came, God's plan would be for him to choose one woman with whom he would spend the rest of his life caring for, loving, respecting, and protecting.

Another friend of ours has a son who started out with light fingers and little impulse control. As cute as he was, we'd have to pat him down whenever he left our house after a play date. He'd inevitably have one or two of Mark's little toys tucked into his pockets. No one had ever taught this child to steal; it was a tendency born within him. As with Mark's inbred tendency to charm and flirt, our job—that is, as parents and our surrounding "village"—was to train them to know that their natural tendencies were not okay.

If you didn't start monitoring your kids' tendencies at infancy, don't fret about it. They have simply grown taller. In most cases, they haven't grown out of their early propensities. You can still see them if you're brave enough to admit that they are there. Now that you're dealing with young adults, your battle plan will have to be a little different, but the goal is still the same. Instead of helping your child in small steps and by casual yet consistent comments, you'll have to tackle the issues head-on.

If your daughter's a people pleaser and your son's a procrastinator, point it out directly. If your son's a flirt and your daughter's a spendthrift, tell them that you notice. If your daughter's shyness is hampering her advancement or your son's fears are holding him back, note and reveal what you are seeing. These conversations must be conducted in a loving manner, or your goal of growth and change will not be met.

Approaching tough, personal character issues doesn't have to be a daunting task. Here are some easy steps to make those conversations run smoothly.

1. Remember with whom you are dealing. This is the child you have loved since infancy. It's your love that's fueling the conversation, not your frustration.
2. Keep your goal in mind. The goal is to have your child recognize the weakness or propensity that is a hindrance. Together, you will attack and conquer the problematic penchant, not the person.
3. Phrase your opening statements in the first person rather than in the second. Say something like, "I have some success secrets that I'd like to share. I'm available on Tuesday and Thursday evening this week. Which one should we choose?" By emphasizing "I" rather then "you," protective walls won't go up as quickly. It doesn't sound like you're ready to pounce, and it suggests that something positive will be discussed.
4. Before you meet for the talk, pray. Ask God to intervene so that you are clearly understood, and so that your child can clearly communicate his or her thoughts as well.

5. Also before you meet, write down the specific concern that you'd like to discuss. Keep your list short. One character trait at a time is enough for one conversation.
6. During the talk, gently mention the tendency that is of central concern. Discuss one or two proofs that have caused you to believe that it's a problem. Show evidence of the destruction at the end of the road if this issue is not rectified. Then propose some achievable adjustments.
7. Allow your child to respond. Hopefully, he or she has been enlightened and can articulate not only understanding of what you have said, but also agreement that some changes should be made.
8. Write down some steps to reach the desired goal. Set some dates. Both of you sign this and pray over it. This paper now becomes the contractual arrangement between you, your child, and God to at least get started toward the positive character development necessary.

It's altogether possible that steps 6 through 8 won't happen in just one conversation. Be patient and prayerful. The worrisome tendencies have been allowed to take root over the years, and so the roots may well be difficult to unearth.

## Avoid Babying

Even when they were babies, I didn't talk to my kids in baby talk. "Coochie-coochie-coo" was never in my vocabulary. As both an educator and a parent, I think that it's healthy to speak to children using regular and correct English. Not only will they grow up speaking correctly and with the ability to communicate intelligibly, but also they will transition more easily into the various stages of their maturity.

Now, I'm not advocating that we tell little children all about adult issues; however, speaking with them using proper English is just one step toward conditioning ourselves to speak with them properly in other situations as well. Children can understand more than we give them credit for comprehending. They internalize how we speak to them, what they hear around them, and what we allow from them.

I remember the first time I heard Mark say a curse word. He was five years old and had been playing with some of the neighborhood children out in the front yard. Someone had been hit by a ball and responded with a curse word. Later that evening, Mark bumped into something and responded with the same word that he had heard. We knew that he hadn't heard that word from our mouths; he had simply internalized it and how to use it from what he had observed outside. Hearing a five-year-old curse wasn't "cute," but he wasn't cursing maliciously. Enter a teachable moment. I asked him where he had heard that word and explained that that word was called a "curse word." After an explanation about how God didn't want any corrupt communication coming from our lips (see Ephesians 4:29), he understood that he would now need to guard against using such words.

If we don't baby our kids when they're small, they won't expect to be babied when they're young adults.

I have come to suspect that many of my male high school students have been babied. During their senior year they become very uncomfortable about graduating. They realize that they are not the "men" everyone told them they would be the moment they turned eighteen. They are suddenly expected to take on the responsibility of protecting our nation, become totally responsible for their own actions, live on their own (caring for all their personal needs such as food, shelter, clothing), and even possibly provide for a wife and children.

The shock and awe occur especially in the guys whose mothers have always done everything for them. Mistakenly thinking that they were helping smooth their sons' way through life, those moms instead hindered their sons' ability to grow into the men they needed to be. Now the moms seemed like traitors to the young men, suddenly casting them out there into a world they knew nothing about. Their gender, deep voice, and some innate survival instinct were somehow supposed to automatically kick in, but the boys were nervous. Some of them even saw themselves as disappointments to their moms because they were sincerely expected to just be ready to be men.

Girls who had been babied seem to get away with it a little longer, but the negative side of this catches up with them eventually. Babied young women can turn their dependent habits into detrimental coyness with the opposite sex. They have learned well how to get what they want from mommy and daddy (usually from daddy), and now they use those techniques on the men they meet. Sadly for the daughter you have babied, men can spot a brat from miles away, and knowing how to get what they want from a spoiled young woman, they spend a little cash and then move on to the next victim, shattering your daughter's heart into a million pieces.

From just these two examples, we should be convinced of the devastation that can be caused when we baby our children. I'm not advocating that we never hug them and cuddle with them. Our kids need quality, close time with us as we teach them the balance between the right and wrong kinds of love. However, we ought to also be intentional about letting them grow up, teaching them how to detect and form safe relationships, and allowing them to gain the tools necessary to be ready to live independently.

The college years are a great transitional time. Living away at school gives our kids the best of both worlds. They are living outside of our homes, far enough away to allow them to practice this newly found independence, yet attached enough to still need pretty regular dialogue that we can use as checkpoints. Terri Lynn Lomax, a young lady I met at a conference when she was twenty-one, shared with me what I consider to be an excellent outlook on this time of her life:

> My little six-year-old brother, Terry, and I had a conversation about adulthood versus childhood. He came to the conclusion that adults are boring, and that children are much more fun. I told him that he was correct, and that I knew firsthand because I am an adult. He looked up at me with bright innocent eyes and asked curiously, "If you're a grown up, then why are you living in our house?"

> The reason why I am currently living at home is because I am finishing up my undergraduate career, which puts me in no position to support myself independently. Eighty percent of the year I live on-campus (one hour and thirty minutes from home), and I only go home on weekends, holidays, and mandatory breaks. My parents sympathize with the level of impoverishment that I am experiencing as a college student; thus, they have allowed me to stay at their home for as long as I desire.
>
> Although I am exceedingly grateful for my parents' generosity, I believe that I should move out shortly after graduation. My goal is to attend graduate school, and I think that as an adult, it would be appropriate for me to get out in the "real world," find a source of income, and fend for myself. My parents have done more than enough for me and at this point in my life, I would actually be sort of embarrassed to be freeloading off of them while I am a competent adult who can work and survive on my own.

Again, college is a great transitional time from childhood to adulthood. The college experience represents a period of growth, socialization, and wisdom. Students in dormitories are monitored by and are responsible to resident advisors (RAs), and faculty members and administrators invest in their students by nurturing abilities and values that hopefully will carry on after graduation.

Although many families allow their young adults to choose the universities that they want to attend, it's still a good idea to be behind the scenes, checking the atmosphere of the institutions into which they are probing. We're simply expressing our natural concerns, not babying our young adults, when, in addition to our child's desire to attend a particular college, we factor in other issues besides cost and the academic majors offered.

»»» **PARENTAL PAUSE:** When it's time to send your child away to college (and I highly recommend that you do), get the low-down on the university.

- Is it known as a "party school"?
- Are there Christian clubs on campus of which your child may become a part?
- Does the atmosphere encourage or discourage Christian expression?

- Are there any restrictions on freshman activities, and are there curfews for dormitory residents?
- Are there coed dorms? If so, are the guys and girls separated wing by wing, floor by floor, or simply room by room?
- How are safety issues handled on campus?

## Avoid Enabling

The final area of watchfulness for us to look at is that of enabling. If we aren't careful, our sense of concern for our children's well-being will slide into a habit of enabling.

According to Beth McHugh, an enabler is "a person who recognizes that a negative circumstance is occurring on a regular basis and yet inadvertently assists the person with the problem to persist with their detrimental behaviors."[1] This term usually is assigned to people who refuse to see the problem of drug abuse or alcoholism in a loved one, but the term can be very effectively applied to our parenting. By continually doing for our kids that which they should be learning to do for themselves, we are functioning as enablers, enabling them to remain immature and poorly equipped for independence.

Now, granted, the line between enabling and supporting our young adults can be quite thin, severely blurred, and sometimes subjective. For example, arguments can be made on both sides when we discuss such questions as whether or not to finance a daughter's visits to the beauty salon or a son's trips home for Thanksgiving and spring break. Some would say that these expenses are simply part of the parents' support and should remain their responsibility during the college years because mom and dad were financing these things before. Others would argue that learning responsibility should include earning one's own money for things such as personal upkeep and optional trips.

Whether we agree or not on the specifics, it's still important for us to understand what enabling behavior is, and to realize that it has proven to be detrimental to the one enabled. If our children refuse to move into adulthood, it shouldn't be because we have enabled their underdevelopment.

Dr. Phil McGraw offers a self-test to answer the question "Are you an enabler?" The quiz originally was put forth to see whether or not the person reading it was assisting a chemically dependent loved one, but I believe that it can be adapted for use as an excellent checklist to test whether or not we are enabling our children to remain dependent and immature, thus setting them up to be future boomerangs. With the original article[2] adapted for our purposes, the introduction and the list would read as follows:

> An enabler is a person who, acting out of a sincere sense of love, loyalty and concern, steps in to protect, cover up for, make excuses for and become more responsible for the dependent young adult. This can prevent the boomerang, dependent child from the crisis that might bring about change, and thereby prolong his or her residence in our home. Some common enabling behaviors are:
>
> - Avoiding problems by trying to keep the peace.
> - Believing that a lack of conflict will solve problems.
> - Denying that the person is refusing to take responsibility for himself or herself.
> - Keeping your feelings inside.
> - Minimizing: "It's not so bad, things will get better when. . . ."
> - Lecturing, blaming, or criticizing the child who is refusing to grow up and move on.
> - Taking over his or her responsibilities.
> - Protecting the boomerang child from pain.
> - Feeling superior; continuing to treat the boomerang young adult like a child.
> - Not taking control of the dependent person.
> - Enduring: "This too shall pass."
> - Waiting: "God will take care of this."

It's hard to hear, but the bottom line is this: we are not doing our young adults a favor when we help them remain immature, underdeveloped, and dependent upon us to meet all or most of their needs. We love our kids, but we simply have to let them grow up. Wouldn't we all like to live with someone who cooks our meals (only the things we like to eat!), washes our clothes, cleans our rooms, makes our beds, and pays our way? Show me where to sign up! No wonder our boomerangs are comfortably living with us without any serious thought or plan of leaving any time soon.

Our children can't be expected to learn in one day what they are to do as independent adults. They won't learn the day after high school graduation, the year after, or even their senior year of college. We didn't learn it all at once, either. However, we do our young adults a huge disservice when we do not start early, or if we refuse to start now, to teach them about what's going to be expected of them as self-regulating, self-sufficient, and beneficially contributing members of society.

**NOTES**

1. Beth McHugh, "Are You an Enabler?" *Families.com*, June 18, 2006, http://www.families.com/blog/are-you-an-enabler (accessed June 3, 2013).

2. Phil McGraw, "Are You an Enabler?" *DrPhil.com*, http://drphil.com/articles/article/680/ (accessed June 3, 2013).

CHAPTER 6

# Broken Arrows »»»

In vain you . . .
stay up late.

PSALM 127:2a

Just as it is vain to rise up early, as we saw in the preceding chapter, so also it is vain to stay up late. However, when God is in control, the Lord may have some late work in mind for us. The "late work" is the continued work that we may have to do with our children after they have reached young adult age. Sometimes it's necessary to pitch in and help adult children in extenuating circumstances—when they are broken arrows—even to the point of them coming back home. Their issues may be financial, emotional, or physical, and each unique context requires a tailored response. Thankfully, the word of God speaks to this state of affairs just as it speaks to every other situation that might come into our lives. The first most important thing that we can do for our broken arrows is uplift them by helping them identify more closely with Jesus.

## The Bible's Boomerangs

The Bible tells us stories about boomerang kids. In a sense, Jesus is a boomerang! Look at it this way: He left his heavenly Father's house and moved in with a young couple that wasn't even married yet. Once he'd been there for thirty years, he roamed around with twelve guys teaching them all that he knew. When one of those guys betrayed him to his enemies, all his friends forsook him, and the bullies beat him up so badly that he finally went back home.

Jesus, of course, embodies a unique set of circumstances. Being God in the flesh, he was supposed to go back home to heaven. But when he returned home, he was equal to His Father. He reigned once again in the eternal glory that he had laid aside in order to redeem us. While he was away from home, he never became less than who he always was. While on earth, he constrained his magnificence to put on the flesh that became our sin. In this way, he murdered our sin when he died on the cross. By doing so, he opened the way to heaven for us.

Our broken arrows can begin their restoration by moving closer and closer to Jesus.

»»» **PARENTAL PAUSE:** Read the following verses to remind yourself of what Jesus has done for you and your children.

- "For Christ also suffered once for sins, the righteous for the unrighteous, to bring you to God. He was put to death in the body but made alive in the Spirit" (1 Peter 3:18, NIV).
- "God made him who had no sin to be sin for us, so that in him we might become the righteousness of God" (2 Corinthians 5:21, NIV).
- "For what the law was powerless to do because it was weakened by the flesh, God did by sending his own Son in the likeness of sinful flesh to be a sin offering. And so he condemned sin in the flesh, in order that the righteous requirement of the law might be fully met in us, who do not live according to the flesh but according to the Spirit" (Romans 8:3–4, NIV).

It is to Christ that we are ultimately pointing our young adults. His death for them means that they can live for him, either as independent adults or in their boomerang state. Wherever they find themselves, their first goal is to exist in the center of his will for them.

If our children boomerang from dependence upon us to quasi–self-sufficiency and back again, they sometimes are unable to focus on God and the fact that the Lord has a plan for their lives.

Helping our boomerangs focus on Jesus is the first step toward depressurizing the whole situation. A young adult who is focused on Christ will begin to see the pieces of his or her life drop into place. Lots of the disturbing issues, such as negative attitudes, disrespectful tones, and even hopelessness, will be dissolved by the joy of the Lord and hope in God's guidance. Jesus fulfilled his job here on earth, and that's exactly what we want our children to do with their lives. Using the first few weeks of the broken arrow's return to focus on a relationship with Christ should help set the tone for the rest of his or her temporary stay.

Let's take a look at two more Bible boomerangs, whose cases aren't quite so unique as that of Jesus.

## When the Fall Is the Kid's Fault: The Prodigal Son

The first case involves a character from one of the most popular stories of the New Testament: the prodigal son. Like this young man, sometimes our children make mistakes. (I know, it hurts to admit it, but here we are!) At other times, bad things just happen to them. In either case, the old adage is true and applies here: the bigger they are, the harder they fall. Whether they're big by virtue of their height, life position, or ego, big people fall hard. And when falls aren't fatal, the fallen usually need stitches, not slaps. The prodigal son took a fall that was his own fault, so we'll look at him first. Here's a portion of the story that Jesus told, from Luke 15:

> There was a man who had two sons. The younger one said to his father, "Father, give me my share of the estate." So he divided his property between them.
>
> Not long after that, the younger son got together all he had, set off for a distant country and there squandered his wealth in wild living. After he had spent everything, there was a severe famine in that whole country, and he began to be in need. So he went and hired himself out to a citizen of that country, who sent him to his fields to feed pigs. He longed to fill his stomach with the pods that the pigs were eating, but no one gave him anything.
>
> When he came to his senses, he said, "How many of my father's hired servants have food to spare, and here I am starving to death! I

> will set out and go back to my father and say to him: Father, I have sinned against heaven and against you. I am no longer worthy to be called your son; make me like one of your hired servants." So he got up and went to his father.
>
> But while he was still a long way off, his father saw him and was filled with compassion for him; he ran to his son, threw his arms around him and kissed him.
>
> The son said to him, "Father, I have sinned against heaven and against you. I am no longer worthy to be called your son."
>
> But the father said to his servants, "Quick! Bring the best robe and put it on him. Put a ring on his finger and sandals on his feet. Bring the fattened calf and kill it. Let's have a feast and celebrate. For this son of mine was dead and is alive again; he was lost and is found." So they began to celebrate. (Luke 15:11-24, NIV)

Like the prodigal fellow of this story, our children are likely to do some stupid things with their (or our) money. (With very few exceptions, we parents made some stupid monetary choices when we were young, so please keep that in mind.) This story does not excuse this young man. We are shown the error of his ways by the consequences he faced. And that's the first lesson that we parents can take away from this story: when our kids do stupid things with money, we must make the hard yet necessary decision to allow them to face the consequences. When this was allowed for this fellow, he learned several important life lessons:

### *You Can't Buy Friendship*

The passage says that the young man "wasted his possessions with prodigal living." The word "wasted" translates the Greek word *diaskorpizō*, which means "to dissipate, squander, scatter abroad." The King James Version says that the young man wasted his resources in "riotous" living, translating the Greek adverb *asōtōs*, whose noun form is *asōtia*, meaning "profligacy" (cf. Ephesians 5:18; Titus 1:6; 1 Peter 4:4). Frankly, I'd never heard that word before, so I learned from a dictionary that a profligate is a person given to wildly extravagant and usually grossly self-indulgent expenditure. Since people don't generally live wild alone, it's safe to assume that this young man spent all his money by scattering it around, spending it to enjoy himself with new friends and friendly strangers. Once the money was gone, so were the friends, and he found himself alone.

Our prodigals must be allowed to learn that people will use them and then throw them away if they are not wise in selecting their acquaintances. It's hard to let our kids fail, but, unpleasant as it may be to experience, failure can be our best teacher. Once burned, we are slow to put our hands in fire again.

It may be particularly difficult to watch as our young adults are acquainted with unsavory, unscrupulous, and scandalous people. If we've warned them about such folks as they were growing up, they should have a better chance at avoiding these types. However, Christian youngsters especially might have the tendency to be overly trusting. We do want to build within them a confidence in humankind, but a healthy dose of skepticism is great to have once in a while as well.

### *Save—Rainy Days Are Coming*

Once this young man ran out of money and friends, his situation went from bad to worse. A famine hit and he was stuck: no money, no friends, no job, no food. Most of our kids can go a few days without eating. Fasting is actually good for the soul. Rainy-day lessons aren't learned unless you get wet.

When our son Matthew was about to embark upon his senior year of college, he received news from the registrar that he owed additional money for the previous year. Unless he paid it, he would not be allowed to register for the new semester. He called home. Unfortunately, he had spent some money on a new car—money that he could have used to cover his tuition. When I relayed the news that he needed help, my husband said, "Too bad. He has to learn, and don't you help him."

I was devastated. Although I agreed in theory with my husband's reasoning, all I could see was three years of college going down the drain because of a few hundred dollars. I was dedicated to standing united with my husband, but I was sick about not being able to help my son. It was a rainy day, and Matthew was definitely getting wet. (I'll pick up Matthew's story below.)

### *Take What Work You Can Get*

One redeeming quality about the biblical prodigal was that he took whatever work he could find. This fellow "joined himself to a citizen of that country" who gave him the job of feeding the pigs. It was dirty, nasty work, but he did it. It was at this job that he realized how low he had sunk. He found himself actually wanting to eat what the pigs were eating. That's when he "came to himself."

Many of our kids feel that they're too good to do certain jobs. If we rescue our young adults every time they run out of money, they won't know how to rescue themselves and won't develop a balanced perspective on who they really are. Our kids are travelers in this life's journey, just like everyone else. An honest day's work at a morally acceptable job is not beneath any of them. Sure, it's a blessing, through talent, and education, to be in a position to bypass some of the more strenuous or less glamorous jobs, but it is arrogant when we allow our children to judge such work as being beneath them. The problem is that when they do so, they also judge the people who do those jobs as being beneath them as well. Then they're in trouble territory with God for thinking of themselves more highly over others than they ought to (see Romans 12:3).

### *Needs Come before Wants*

I'm grateful to say that our Matthew's situation wasn't one in which he felt too good to work a particular job; he just had to come up with something and fast. Believe me when I tell you, I prayed hard that God would help Matthew figure out what he could do to take care of his tuition. He had started attending a different church from ours closer to his college, so I went to church with him that following Sunday. We knelt together at the altar during their prayer time, and I poured out my heart and tears to God over the situation. I was leaving town to teach at a conference that next day and wouldn't be close to Matthew as he faced the situation.

The following day, as I was teaching a workshop at the conference, Matthew left me a text message. When I got to my phone, I read his note, which simply said, "I'm registered."

I could hardly wait to find out what happened. When I was able to call, he told me that he discovered he could transfer over money from his meal plan to cover his tuition. This solution reduced his meal allowance, but he would be able to earn and save up enough money from his part-time job for food as the new semester rolled along.

On his own, Matthew had figured out how to make things work. He learned that necessities must come before pleasantries, and that doing things the other way around is usually quite costly. He now had to hustle to do whatever work he could get, whether he enjoyed it or not, so that he could eat, but he was registered in that last semester, and that was most important.

### *Parents Are Always There for You—Respect Them*

The prodigal finally "came to himself." He realized two very important things: the necessity of respecting his father, and the fact that his father (parents) would always be there for him.

If our children are to be well-rounded, respectable adults and parents later on in life, they must come to the understanding that their parents really do know important stuff and deserve to be listened to. This presupposes that we parents are indeed honorable (see in chapter 2 the section "Admiration," which talks about honorable parenting). One of the great joys of parenting is doling out sage advice. Smart kids listen and learn.

Let me add that as parents, we earn this respect by dealing with our children in love. Yes, there are times for the heavy hand of tough love (like we used with Matthew), but once the lessons are adequately learned, the time is right for the hand that we used when they were small: the hand that picked them up, brushed them off, and drew them close to help make everything better again. When our kids blow it and learn their lesson, they should still know that mom and dad love them enough to work with them to get them back on their feet.

### *You Need to Acknowledge Your Mistake*

The prodigal son acknowledged that he had blown it, and he decided to return home. All the way home, he practiced the speech that he planned to tell his father: "I am no longer worthy to be called your son." He was ready to take the low place as one of his father's servants, just to be back near the goodness that he once knew. That's true repentance.

That which we refuse to acknowledge can never teach us anything. The fallen kid who refuses to admit failure is simply going to commit the same mistakes, missteps, and misjudgments over and over again. Assisting such a child will very quickly become enabling (see chapter 5). Only the child who can honestly admit his or her own complicity is ready to learn from the mistake and turn things around.

Although we are working our way out of the job as day-to-day providers, as parents of young adult children, we never totally relinquish our title. In the same way as we always see our kids as our kids, they should always see us as their parents. At the same time, both sides must adjust when the children become adults. The kids shouldn't expect the parents to continue to provide; the parents shouldn't expect the kids to continue to do everything they say. When there's a serious-enough issue that necessitates a possible move back home, the adult children must remember they are guests in their parents' home, and behave accordingly. The parents, as well, must remember that their child is now a dependent adult, not a dependent child. Differences exist, but those differences don't outweigh the love that will always stay the same.

Notice the biblical father's response to his broken arrow. First of all, he was expectantly looking for his son to return. The passage says, "But while he was still a long way off, his father saw him." The only way the father could have seen the son when he was still a long way off is if he was looking for his son. Second, he had compassion on his child. The Scripture goes on to say that the father threw off the dignity of his position: "He ran to his son, threw his arms around him and kissed him." Then he didn't even allow the young man to finish his little speech. Without even being asked, the father reached out to help. He celebrated his son's return. There was no need for the "I told you so" speech. The kid already knew that he had blown it. All that was necessary right then was cheer. Fixing things could start later.

Parents, we know when our kids are headed for a fall. If we've fostered an atmosphere of love throughout their lives, we can expect them to return when times get too rough. Our attitude toward our broken arrows should be the same as that of this biblical father: compassion. The word *compassion* means "sympathy and pity." When we're sympathetic, we feel another's pain, and pity carries along with it the yearning to do something to help.

Colossians 3:13 says, "Bear with each other and forgive one another if any of you has a grievance against someone. Forgive as the Lord forgave you" (NIV). Our grown children are our brothers and sisters in Christ. And Ephesians 4:32 reminds us, "Be kind and compassionate to one another, forgiving each another, just as in Christ God forgave you" (NIV).

»»» **PARENTAL PAUSE:** So let's review. The story of the prodigal son offers us a number of checkpoints to look for when young adults feel the need to boomerang back home after making some sort of mistake. Before offering them their old room, check to see if they are:

1. Becoming a better judge of character (see "You Can't Buy Friendship").
2. Committed to financial responsibility (see "Save—Rainy Days Are Coming" and "Needs Come before Wants").
3. Accepting the work that they can get (see "Take What Work You Can Get").
4. Respectful of you (see "Parents Are Always There for You—Respect Them").
5. Honestly acknowledging their mistakes (see "You Need to Acknowledge Your Mistake").

It really doesn't matter what the indiscretion has been. With the lessons learned, we can accept the boomeranging prodigals back. But here's the caveat: broken arrows return to the quiver with the understanding that this living arrangement is temporary, just for an understood and agreed-upon amount of time as we assist them in getting back on their own two feet. Nothing we've discussed in the previous five chapters has changed at all. Young adults need to carry on as the next generation, operating independently of their parents.

### When the Fall Is Not the Kid's Fault: Mephibosheth

Unlike with the prodigal son, sometimes the reason that necessitates a boomerang situation is of no fault of the child. Life happens. The closest biblical example that I could find is in the Old Testament, when Mephibosheth experienced a fall that was not his fault.

We meet Mephibosheth when he is just five years old: "Jonathan son of Saul had a son who was lame in both feet. He was five years old when the news about Saul and Jonathan came from Jezreel. His nurse picked him up and fled, but as she hurried to leave, he fell and became disabled. His name was Mephibosheth" (2 Samuel 4:4, NIV). Unable to care for himself even when he grew older, this boy had to live at home to be taken care of. Since his father, Jonathan, had been killed, King David took on his best friend Jonathan's responsibility as Meshibosheth's foster parent. The rest of the story is told in 2 Samuel 9, but the crux of it is this:

> When Mephibosheth son of Jonathan, the son of Saul, came to David, he bowed down to pay him honor.
>
> David said, "Mephibosheth!"
>
> "At your service," he replied.
>
> "Don't be afraid," David said to him, "for I will surely show you kindness for the sake of your father Jonathan. I will restore to you all the land that belonged to your grandfather Saul, and you will always eat at my table." (2 Samuel 9:6-7, NIV)

Many possible severe circumstances could lead to an adult child's need to move back home. As in Mephibosheth's case, there could be a physical malady or mental condition. Perhaps your daughter has experienced an abusive relationship or marriage, or a divorce has left your son totally devastated. Perhaps an unfortunate disaster such as a fire or a sudden job loss has caused homelessness and severe financial reversal. David's care for Mephibosheth shows us some things about caring for our boomerangs who need to move back home through no fault of their own.

### *The Problem Is Serious*

My very good friend ShaRon Cole experienced a devastating stroke more than a decade ago. Already an independent adult in her early 40s and raising two young adopted daughters, ShaRon fell into the care of her single mother, Jeretta, who took on the full responsibility of all three: her daughter and her two granddaughters. I have heard Jeretta say, "I see God's purpose for my life in taking care of this child." ShaRon's problem was serious, making it necessary to live in her mother's home in order to receive necessary care.

It was touch and go for months following the stroke, but ShaRon has fought back. She is still unable to live independently, but she has rallied back quite a way. The link between thought and communication is broken in her brain, but she's slowly relearning speech, writing, and reading. Jeretta is dedicated to living out the rest of her life caring for her daughter.

Many boomerang situations are not this drastic, but having the "Jeretta attitude" is still necessary when crisis strikes our young-adult kids. In such cases, perhaps God's life purpose for us really is physically caring for the one we brought into the world for the rest of our lives.

Note that, much as could be said about Mephibosheth, ShaRon is high functioning, so moment-to-moment care is actually minimal. More severe physical disabilities may be beyond a parent's ability to personally handle, and we need not feel that God blames us or that we're bad parents when we need the assistance of professional nursing or rehabilitative facilities. We are still fulfilling our obligation to our children by searching out the best care possible.

And let's not overlook mental and emotional disabilities. Usually easier to neglect and ignore, these types of special needs require just as much attention and care as do physical maladies. Excellent information is readily available concerning troubles such as bipolar disorder, anorexia, depression, anxiety, and ADHD, to name just a few.

In a two-parent family, one parent may have a much more difficult time accepting the reality of these disorders than the other. Some of us are more prone to accept the concrete over the abstract; others are vocationally trained for or naturally inclined toward the care required by medical or emotional needs. However, both parents must seek understanding and be just as intentionally dedicated to our mentally and emotionally unbalanced children as we are to those with physical problems.

### *The Place Is Obvious*

Some famous people have said some profound things about home. "Home is where the heart is," said the philosopher Pliny the Elder. The poet Robert Frost declared, "Home is the place where, when you have to go there, they have to take you in." The playwright William Shakespeare observed, "People usually are the happiest at home." And the journalist Helen Rowland proclaimed, "Home is any four walls that enclose the right person."

When something devastating and unforeseen happens to our adult children, the obvious place to which they can (and should be able to) return is home. They can receive protection, as in the case of a daughter escaping an abusive relationship; confidence, such as that needed to bolster a child headed for the twentieth job interview; or encouragement, as may be required for a son recovering from a career-ending sports injury. The décor of the rooms may have changed (we completely remodeled the kids' room when our last one left, but that's another amusing story for another day), but the heart of mom and dad's home remains the same. Until the day we die, parents are first in line with our children's best interest at heart, and when called upon to step in to handle a crisis, we're still there for them.

Another twist on this point is that sometimes our adult children will move back in with us because *we* need *them*. This is technically not a boomerang situation, since boomerang kids are returning because of their needs, not ours. It was actually an honor to move back into my parents' home with my husband and young family when my father was stricken with Alzheimer's and later suffered a stroke. We were there for additional care for him and support for my mother. Daddy also spent precious time with my boys during this last phase of his life.

It's important for us to remember that one day the shoe may be on the other foot. If we have a comfortable home, adequate to meet both our and our adult children's needs, welcoming them back in order to care for us may be a smoother transition if some time in the past they can remember being welcomed back when they were in serious need.

### *The Provision Is Freely Offered*

Parents who realize their children's need and offer to help should do so freely. In other words, we ought to see the need and offer assistance even before the child has to ask for help. This assistance is offered neither as a matter of guilt nor as a matter of negative compulsion. What we're guilted into doing or forced to do, we do begrudgingly. If the time comes for us to offer our children the opportunity to move back in, we should do so with open arms.

Never should we make our suffering adult children feel as though they are a burden to us. (Remember, we're discussing broken arrows in drastic situations.) If their situation can be turned around after a time, sure, we're free to also assist them in getting back on their feet and back into an independent living arrangement. The lines of communication between both parties should remain open and amiable so that if any discomfort arises on either side, issues can be discussed rationally.

### *The Proposal Is Sacrificial*

Our kids might have to bring their kids with them. Most grandparents are hard-pressed to refuse to welcome their grandchildren in, especially if they are being removed from a negative environment. Did you know that 2 Samuel 9:12 notes that Mephibosheth had a young son when David took him in? And recall that my friend ShaRon had two daughters.

Once parents have transitioned into the "empty nest" phase of life, we get used to freedom, and freedom is always tough to give up. That's why it's a sacrifice to move grown kids back home. Often, in addition to the baggage of the problem itself, comes the pitter-patter of other little feet. Count the cost, parents, and don't make the offer unless you are willing to accept the sacrifices with a smile. Space and bathroom time will be severely limited; the electric, water, and grocery bills will be considerably higher; and there will be more dishes and clothes to wash. Who gets to watch what on TV, and how is computer time allocated? And don't forget the noise; little children can make a lot of it.

A delicate balance will also have to be struck if your childrearing philosophies differ from your son's or daughter's. Iron those things out up front. For example, if you believe in spanking and your daughter doesn't, what happens when your three-year-old grandson deliberately dumps the sugar bowl on the newly mopped kitchen floor after you directly told him to stop playing with it?

The bottom line is the Golden Rule. Luke 6:31 clearly states, "Do to others as you would have them do to you" (NIV). We often disregard biblical injunctions when it comes to family members; however, truth must be applied to everyone in the same degree. Both the adult children who return home as broken arrows and the parents who take them in ought to keep this command foremost in their minds. If they do, the arrangement will work well for all concerned.

CHAPTER 7

# Bent Arrows »»»

In vain you . . .
toil for food to eat.

PSALM 127:2c

We have made our way up to the third phrase of verse 2 in our study through Psalm 127 as it relates to our arrows (our children) who have boomeranged back, or who would like to boomerang back, into our homes. For memory's sake, let's look again at those first two verses up to where we are now:

> Unless the LORD builds the house, the builders labor in vain. Unless the LORD watches over the city, the guards stand watch in vain. In vain you rise early and stay up late, toiling for food to eat. (Psalm 127:1-2c, NIV)

Where the New International Version has "toiling for food to eat," the New Revised Standard Version has "eating the bread of anxious toil," an interesting phrase that lends quite a bit of insight to our discussion. Looking at the Hebrew words, we find that the word for "eat" can also mean "to consume, burn up"; the word for "bread" means "bread, food, nourishment," basically that which sustains us; and the word for "anxious toil" means "painful toil of body and mind." As we converse about our young-adult children, then, the psalm is telling us that unless God is taking care of us, it is vain or useless for us to live from day to day being consumed with stress about them.

Many a gospel song has been written about turning problems over to Jesus, placing worries in the Master's hand, and carrying burdens to the Lord. Our problem is not in the turning over of the problems, the placing of the worries, or the taking of the burdens to the Lord. Our problem arises from not *leaving* the problems, worries, and burdens for God to handle. Unfortunately, we are amateurs when it comes to setting ourselves up in the providence business, injecting our know-how into our children's situations when God is the only providential presence they need.

Yes, we hurt when our children hurt. In fact, we hurt before they hurt when we see them rushing headlong into disaster. The daughter always hooking up with the wrong kind of guy, the son wrapped up in pride, the young woman trusting in her money, the young man experimenting with drugs—all of these issues deeply concern us. The arrows that our children should be are sometimes twisted and horribly bent by bad choices, bad character, and bad company. Adult children who are bent on following a course contrary to God's laws will soon find themselves worse off than they could ever imagine. The Bible is replete with warnings about such attitudes. Look at the following examples:

- "There is a way that appears to be right, but in the end it leads to death" (Proverbs 16:25, NIV).
- "The righteous choose their friends carefully, but the way of the wicked leads them astray" (Proverbs 12:26, NIV).
- "The way of fools seems right to them, but the wise listen to advice" (Proverbs 12:15, NIV).
- "You boast, 'We have struck a bargain to cheat death and have made a deal to dodge the grave. The coming destruction can never touch us, for we have built a strong refuge made of lies and deception.' Therefore, this is what the Sovereign Lord says: 'Look! I am placing a foundation stone in Jerusalem, a firm and tested stone. It is a precious cornerstone that is safe to build on. Whoever believes need never be shaken. I will test you with the measuring line of justice and the plumb line of righteousness. Since your refuge is made of lies, a hail-

> storm will knock it down. Since it is made of deception, a flood will sweep it away. I will cancel the bargain you made to cheat death, and I will overturn your deal to dodge the grave. When the terrible enemy sweeps through, you will be trampled into the ground'" (Isaiah 28:15-18, NLT).

From these passages, we can see that if adult children are operating willy-nilly in the world, the truth of two other verses hits us squarely in the face. Proverbs 17:25 says, "Foolish children are a grief to their father and bitterness to her who bore them" (NRSV), and Proverbs 29:15b asserts, "A child left undisciplined disgraces its mother" (NIV).

Without the prayers of our forefathers and foremothers, where would we be? At the point when we can no longer talk to our grown kids, there's only one thing left to do: pray. The one kind of help that doesn't make our children helpless is prayer.

As we pray, we still remain the controllers of what we will and will not allow in our own homes. Adult kids who are involved with us in a power struggle, bound by addictions, intent upon disobeying our rules, and exhibiting a destructive lack of discipline can be shown the door and determinedly directed to find someplace else to live. Your unmarried daughter who boomeranged home with the first baby should be finding an apartment when she turns up pregnant with the second. Your son who insists upon setting up an idol and an altar to his new religion can be told he's welcome to do that in his own place. Refuse to supplement the laziness of your high school sports star who refused the full-ride scholarship to what she called a "no name" university, and decline to support your aspiring actor who is now refusing "menial" jobs because of his new training regimen.

These kids are bent—bent on having their own way, bent on not listening to or following wise counsel, and bent on living off of you. Put them out and pray.

»»» **PARENTAL PAUSE:** What kinds of negative character traits have you been refusing to acknowledge that you clearly see in your child? Admitting the problems that we see is the first step toward relieving them.

## Following Biblical Parents

The Bible tells us of several parents who took their problems about their children to God. In the Gospels, we see parents begging Jesus to heal or cast demons out of their kids. In my opinion, the Old Testament holds the consummate story of a mother who exercised her faith before God concerning her child. In the book of 2 Kings, we read the story of the Shunammite woman and learn three important principles about approaching God with problems regarding our children.

This Shunammite woman was so hospitable to Elisha that she had her husband add a room to their home to house the prophet whenever he passed through town. Realizing that she had no children and her husband was old, to thank her, God allowed Elisha to promise the woman a son. Sure enough, in about a year, the woman had a son. Some years later, while working with his father, the boy began to have terrible pain in his head. When taken to his mother, she helplessly held him while he died. I'll let the Scripture pick the story up from there:

> She called her husband and said, "Please send me one of the servants and a donkey so I can go to [Elisha] the man of God quickly and return."...
>
> She saddled the donkey and said to her servant, "Lead on; don't slow down for me unless I tell you." So she set out and came to the man of God at Mount Carmel....
>
> When she reached the man of God at the mountain, she took hold of his feet. Gehazi came over to push her away, but the man of God said, "Leave her alone! She is in bitter distress, but the LORD has hidden it from me and has not told me why."
>
> "Did I ask you for a son, my lord?" she said. "Didn't I tell you, 'Don't raise my hopes'?"...
>
> The child's mother said, "As surely as the LORD lives and as you live, I will not leave you." So he got up and followed her....
>
> When Elisha reached the house, there was the boy lying dead on his couch. He went in, shut the door on the two of them, and prayed to the LORD. Then he got on the bed and lay on the boy, mouth to mouth, eyes to eyes, hands to hands. As he stretched himself out

> on him, the boy's body grew warm. Elisha turned away and walked back and forth in the room and then got on the bed and stretched out on him once more. The boy sneezed seven times and opened his eyes.
>
> Elisha summoned Gehazi and said, "Call the Shunammite." And he did. When she came, he said, "Take your son." She came in, fell at his feet and bowed to the ground. Then she took her son and went out. (2 Kings 4:22-37, NIV)

Here was a mother who clearly understood that her child was a gift from God. When his illness was not something that she could nurse him through, she raced straight to Elisha, the prophet of God, for help. What are the three principles about taking our children before the Lord that we can learn from this lady?

First, she understood that her child was a gift from God. When God gives us gifts, we ought to treasure them. I still have some gifts that I received many years ago. No matter how shabby they become over time, they will remain precious to me. Their shabbiness means only that these items need that much more special handling. I might have to place a certain item in a protective glass case to preserve it, but you can bet that I will never throw it away.

The same is true for our wayward boomerangs. We still treasure them, and they're still extremely precious and priceless; however, it may just be that their shabbiness will require the special handling of placing them somewhere other than our home. If they stay with us, they're liable to destroy the fabric of the family by their cantankerous and unruly spirit. We call this type of special handling "tough love."

Second, she realized that her only hope for his survival rested in the work of God. Even though her boy was dead, she still held out hope. She was so determined to get help from God that she told Elisha, "As surely as the LORD lives and as you live, I will not leave you." She seemed to have reasoned in her heart, *Elisha's God promised the boy to me; Elisha's God can restore the boy to me.*

Finally, she determined to place her trust in the outcome from God. The reality was extremely clear: her son was dead. But to her, a stronger reality existed: God was alive. Before Elisha was aware of her problem, her response when Elisha's servant

Gehazi inquired about her family was, "Everything is all right" (2 Kings 4:26). She didn't ignore the reality; she did go to Elisha for help. However, she didn't let the condition of her son block out the certainty of her faith.

»»» **PARENTAL PAUSE:** Let's learn from the Shunammite woman and use her wisdom and faith to pray for our own kids. Here's a sample for how we can turn her principles into our prayer. Fill in your child's name and specific situation:

> Dear God, I realize that (child's name) is a gift from you. Although my child is trapped by (child's issue, problem, or illness), all is well. I will not let you go until you come along with me and show your presence in my child's life. Touch, Lord. Heal, Lord. Deliver, Lord. Set free, Lord. I am trusting in your answer for (child's name). In Jesus' name, Amen.

## Model Prayer for Boomerangs-Turned-Arrows

We can extract truths from many biblical stories and apply those truths to our prayer life, but what better prayer to pray over our children than the one outlined by Jesus himself? When the disciples asked Jesus to teach them how to pray, he said, "This, then, is how you should pray: 'Our Father in heaven, hallowed be your name, your kingdom come, your will be done, on earth as it is in heaven. Give us today our daily bread. And forgive us our debts, as we also have forgiven our debtors. And lead us not into temptation, but deliver us from the evil one. For yours is the kingdom and the power and the glory forever'" (Matthew 6:9–13, NIV [including marginal note b]). We can use eight phrases from this prayer as a guide to praying for the boomerangs in our lives, whom we want to become arrows:

### *Our Father in Heaven*

The first thing we want to make sure we're doing is praying to the right person. When we go to God about our kids, it's important to be certain within ourselves that God has the answers that we need and the power to affect change. Psalm 147:5 says, "Great is our LORD and mighty in power; his understanding has no limit" (Psalm 147:5, NIV).

Even though you are reading this book, my desire is that these pages are simply pointing you to the real source of your power: God through the word found in the Bible. Television talk-show hosts, Eastern mysticism gurus, horoscopes, even advice columnists or the family's favorite know-it-all "Great-Aunt Sue"—all may have some good points, but none of the advice from these "experts" should supersede what God has to tell us. When we pray to God, we must be sure that we're praying to the God of the Bible—the God who created heaven and earth, parted the sea, and raised Jesus from the dead. To know God is not only to love God, but also to obey. Our link to God through Jesus Christ gives us the right to approach the Lord with our needs.

Be encouraged, parents, knowing that we can avoid "eating the bread of anxious toil" in regard to our children as we pray to the God of the Bible, the God who can make a difference, the God with whom we have a relationship. The apostle Paul tells us, "So in Christ Jesus you are all children of God through faith, for all of you who were baptized into Christ have clothed yourselves with Christ. . . . If you belong to Christ, then you are Abraham's seed, and heirs according to the promise" (Galatians 3:26-27, 29, NIV). And Jesus says, "If you remain in me and my words remain in you, ask whatever you wish, and it will be done for you. This is to my Father's glory, that you bear much fruit, showing yourselves to be my disciples. As the Father has loved me, so have I loved you. Now remain in my love. If you keep my commands, you will remain in my love, just as I have kept my Father's commands and remain in his love" (John 15:7-10, NIV).

### *Hallowed Be Your Name*

Pray that our children will recognize the holiness of God's name and what being called by that name means. We can pray specifically over what our young adults are choosing to do with their lives.

God's name is holy, so as you pray, thank God for reminding your adult children that their lifestyle is to line up with being identified with that name.

### *Your Kingdom Come, Your Will Be Done, on Earth as It Is in Heaven*

Pray that your child will relinquish his or her will to God. Once our children are young adults, we're often no longer involved in their decision-making process. However, especially if we are dealing with boomerang kids, their decisions still directly affect us. Make it a matter of prayer that your children will make God a central part of every decision in which they are involved.

A friend's daughter experiences the highs and lows of schizophrenia. Although living on her own, her parents worry about the decisions that she might make when experiencing either extreme. The most they can do for her is pray. They pray that she will stay consistent with her medication. They pray that the lines of communication will stay open between her and them so that they can detect when her mood is swinging. But most of all, they pray that she will recognize her own connection with God so that she can determine the Lord's will when choices of any kind present themselves.

### *Give Us Today Our Daily Bread*

Pray that God will supply your child's needs. This is probably the easiest part of applying this prayer model to our boomerang kids. If you're anything like me, you've approached God's throne on a daily basis on behalf of your kids ever since you became a parent. Now that those kids are grown, don't stop asking. Pray that God will fulfill both general and specific needs.

Everyone's schedule is packed these days, and mine is no exception. With my husband, my church participation, my teaching job, my writing and speaking ministry, and my seminar schedule, not to mention the relaxation that I'd like to have occasionally with friends, time is of the essence. Still, I know that I'd be good for none of these things without making quality moments with God my first priority. Besides daily Bible reading and special prayer time that's specifically set aside, I was challenged by the Scripture that says, "Pray without ceasing" (1 Thessalonians 5:17, NKJV). I decided to put that into practice praying for our kids. So as I am commuting on California freeways and streets almost every day, I have coupled my driving time with a prayer habit. Every time I see a car of the same make and model that the kids drive, I send up a prayer for them. So, for example, as I pass a Ford Focus, I say, "Lord, bless Matthew." When a Dodge Charger whizzes by me, I declare, "Lord, keep Mark safe." Every Chrysler 300 I see is accompanied by a prayer for Lori, and the Cadillac reminds me to ask God to watch over and take care of Jerod.

Use any little reminder to prompt prayer for your kids as well. When you see a McDonalds® restaurant, pray for the son who always wanted French fries. Whenever you come to a stop sign, send up a petition for the daughter who loves the color red. Any hint will do, as long as you know that you'll see what you've chosen often enough to cause you to pray continually.

If necessary, in an effort to let your children know that it's God who supplies their daily needs, the Lord may have to make those needs scarce in order to become large in their lives. We don't wish tough times on our children, but God loves them too much to let them believe the lie that anyone or anything is better at caring for them. In order for this realization to take hold of them, the Lord may need to block every avenue of fulfillment other than God. As the old saying goes, "We don't really know that God is all we need until God is all we've got." If God is dealing with our children by withholding blessing for a time, keep praying. Don't thwart God's plan and shorten God's hand by stepping in to be your child's source of supply. God is wise beyond our understanding. God is giving them their daily bread by taking them to a place where they can receive sustenance only from God.

### *Forgive Us Our Debts, as We Have Also Forgiven Our Debtors*

Pray that our children will be forgiven and have forgiving spirits. This speaks to our children's humility and general attitude in relation to responding to others. A person who understands what it's like to be forgiven understands what it means to struggle with sin. Knowing about sin, its character, and its consequences is the first step to conquering its strongholds. The forgiven child, aware of his or her own proclivities, is one who is in the right position to grow in the Lord. And such a forgiven child can be a forgiver of others, a humble soul who can show compassion to fellow human beings.

### *Lead Us Not into Temptation*

Pray that your children will not develop damaging addictive habits or dangerous negative associations. Destructive addictions and unprincipled associates can lead our children away from following God's day-by-day directions.

A prayer that I started praying over my children when they were little was, "Lord, if they are doing something wrong, let them get caught the first time." This very simple prayer may sound cruel at first, but think back. Think of a bad habit that you developed. The first time you did it, you felt bad, your stomach churned with butterflies, and you worried about being found out. When nothing happened, although you still looked around cautiously, the next time you did it, your conscience didn't bother you quite as much. It was even easier to carry out the third time. After a while, although the nature of the sinful act didn't change, you no longer felt bad about participating. You probably even started to publicly defend your actions. However, if you had been caught and stopped the first time, that bad habit wouldn't be costing you the time, money, and consequences that you're dealing with today. This truth is supported by Ecclesiastes 8:11: "When the sentence for a crime is not quickly carried out, people's hearts are filled with schemes to do wrong" (NIV).

### *Deliver Us from the Evil One*

Speaking of schemes, pray that your children are protected from that old, slimy schemer, the devil. If you don't believe in the devil anymore, have a look at Ephesians 6:11-12: "Put on the full armor of God, so that you can take your stand against the devil's schemes. For our struggle is not against flesh and blood, but against the rulers, against the authorities, against the powers of this dark world and against the spiritual forces of evil in the heavenly realms" (NIV).

Our young adults are prime targets for Satan, and he works constantly—twenty-four hours a day, seven days a week, 365 days a year, with no rest on leap years—to try to destroy them. And if he can break up the family in the process, he's even more delighted. This fact supplies all the more reason to pray this part of the prayer over your boomerangs.

It's tough if not impossible to gauge the inner beliefs of a non-communicative young adult. Even one who talks with you rather regularly may not be telling you all that he or she is thinking. Listen carefully when your young adult talks. Even silences can be telling. What is this young person coming to believe or disbelieve, accept or reject, stay quiet about or speak up about? Nip in the bud thoughts that are swerving away from God's thoughts.

According to Dr. Frank Turek, in an article at *CrossExamined.org*, "We have a problem in America." The article lists the following statistics and facts:

- 70–75 percent of Christian youth leave the church after high school (according to Barna data and *USA Today*).
- Intellectual skepticism is one of the major reasons they walk away.
- Most Christian students are not equipped to resist rabidly anti-Christian college professors who are intent on converting their students to atheism.
- College professors are five times more likely to identify themselves as atheists than the general public, and more than half of all college professors view evangelical Christian students unfavorably.
- The "new atheists"—Richard Dawkins, Sam Harris, Christopher Hitchens—are writing books and are growing in popularity.[1]

Dr. Turek explains, "The reason for this exodus is that Christian youth in America are not being taught to cross-examine the skeptical and atheistic views they encounter when they leave home."[2]

Why else are young people leaving the church? According to Dr. Turek,

> Some think church is irrelevant. Others, out on their own for the first time, are attracted by all the world has to offer and put God on the back burner. Yet many leave because they've come to doubt Christianity. In fact, intellectual skepticism is a major reason cited by those who have left. Now less than one percent of adults in America have a Biblical worldview!
>
> We can lay the blame for much of this on ourselves—that is, on the church. While there are notable exceptions, most American churches overemphasize emotion and ignore the biblical commands to develop the mind (1 Peter 3:15; 2 Corinthians 10:5). In other words, we're doing a great job performing for our youth with skits, bands, and videos, but a terrible job informing them with logic, truth, and a Christian worldview.[3]

These sentiments are further described in a *USA Today* article by Cathy Lynn Grossman. She quotes Ed Stetzer, director of Nashville-based LifeWay Research, which is affiliated with the publishing arm of the Southern Baptist Convention: "Too many youth groups are holding tanks with pizza. There's no life transformation taking place. People are looking for a faith that can change them and to be a part of changing the world."[4]

Satan rarely springs a frontal attack. He plots and plans and then weasels his way into our thoughts little by little. Pray that God will expose any way the enemy is sneaking in to steal your young-adult boomerang's mind.

### *Yours Is the Kingdom and the Power and the Glory Forever*

Pray that your children will learn to rely on God's power and give the glory due to the Lord. Boomerangs won't learn to rely on God if they can get everything they need by relying on their parents.

It's foolish and futile for us to be "eating the bread of anxious toil," worrying about our kids, when all we have to do is turn them over to God. The Lord really can care for them better than we ever could.

**NOTES**

1. Frank Turek, "Youth Exodus Problem," *CrossExamined.org*, n.d., http://crossexamined.org/youth-exodus-problem/ (accessed June 4, 2013).
2. Ibid.
3. Ibid.
4. Cathy Lynn Grossman, "Young Adults Aren't Sticking with the Church," *USA Today*, March 19, 2011, http://usatoday30.usatoday.com/printedition/life/20070807/d_churchdropout07.art.htm (accessed June 4, 2013).

CHAPTER 8

# Well-Balanced Bows for Our Arrows »»»

For the LORD grants
sleep to those he loves.

PSALM 127:2d

We've spent the past four chapters discussing our arrows, be they quivered, sanded, broken, or bent. Let's take a break here to concentrate again on ourselves, the archers, using our bows (our outlook, our parenting style, our philosophy, etc.) to send our kids into their adulthood. Are our bows balanced?

As we get more and more deeply involved in the parenting process, we can find ourselves losing sleep, tossing and turning, and questioning our parenting skills. The techniques that worked on us simply aren't effective with this generation. We can't seem to understand how these kids think. (Oh my goodness, didn't that sound like something your parents used to say? Welcome to Parenting Reality 101!) We're probably especially dumbfounded to look around and find that the years have quickly passed, and we have grown kids still living at home, young adults who seem like they're never going to mature. We ask ourselves, "Am I doing the right thing by my children? Am I doing enough or too much for them? Was I there for them enough as they were growing up? Have I been too harsh or too lenient?"

I spoke in chapter 4 about how wrapped up I was in my first baby's care. You haven't heard it all. I'm surprised I didn't lose more friends besides the one I mentioned. Determined to give Matthew the healthiest environment imaginable, I insisted upon using cloth diapers so that his delicate skin could breathe. I was also determined never to supplement his diet with store-bought, packaged baby formula. And forget about holding him if you were wearing clothes that had been dry-cleaned. He might rub his cheek against your clothes and breathe in those chemicals. With all due respect, that would never do. I was not going to be the one to blame for his skin rash, obesity, or bad teeth.

I continued nursing Matthew for ten months and even made fruit drinks for him with my juicer, but the cloth diaper service was soon beat out by disposable convenience, and the fear of dry-cleaning chemicals dissipated. In other words, I loosened up; I relaxed. I gave myself permission to care about what I deemed important, but without being excessive or perfect. (Funny how I was the only one requiring that of me.) Matthew got sick sometimes because germs exist. He fell and received scratches and bruises because toddlers are unsteady when they walk. He was appropriately disciplined when he did something wrong because all kids are human beings who make mistakes and disobey the rules. Those sicknesses, scratches, and scoldings were not the result of faulty parenting on my part; they were the natural consequences growing up.

This chapter will talk about letting go of the guilt that parents feel about adult children's mistakes or failures. One of the older ladies from our church had 9 children. Herself a stalwart Christian, some of her children followed the straight and narrow, and some didn't. Although hurt by the waywardness of some of her brood, she understood the adage she often repeated to us younger moms: People gonna do what they're gonna do. This does not excuse us from being the best parents we can be, but it's important to remember that our adult children's foibles are their own, and so must be the consequences if they are ever going to reach maturity. We ought to feel guilty only about wrongs that we've personally committed. When we're feeling guilty over troubles that other people have, the problem is not them, but us. Perhaps (and this might be a bit hard to swallow) our boomerangs are still home more because of our guilt than for their good.

## The Boomerang Entitlement

Almost every website and article I read discussing the issue of boomerang kids cited the economy as the central cause. If that were the case, then what's up with the attitude of many boomerangs who have harsh feelings of blame toward their parents because of their own predicament? I've discovered that some parents are allowing their grown kids to stay or move back home not only because of personal feelings of inadequacy as parents, but also because their kids are telling them they are owed this privilege.

Just recently, I heard a parent remark that her eighteen-year-old daughter's justification for not doing better in high school was this: "All my friends' parents saved thousands of dollars for them to go away to college." This comment, of course, was meant as a backhand slap and transference of blame. Translation: "Since you couldn't afford to send me to an expensive out-of-state school, you stunted my motivation. Thus, it's your fault that I can't find a job to support my independence, living in the manner to which I have become accustomed."

Some young adults also seem to have perfected the art of being passive-aggressive. This type of behavior is characterized by indirect resistance to the demands of others and an avoidance of direct confrontation. It pertains to behavior in which feelings of aggression are expressed in passive ways—for example, stubbornness, sullenness, pouting, procrastination, careless organization or outright disorganization, and intentional inefficiency. Sound familiar?

I was surprised to hear about one of our sons' friends who was getting away with passive-aggressive behavior in his parents' home. From an intact, hard-working family, this fellow wasn't a bad student in high school. His older sister had received her college degree and was off on her own, and his younger sister had plans to attend a state school to pursue nursing. This young man should have been graduating from college. Instead, I was shocked to discover that he had spent the past four years just sitting around his parents' house during the day and hanging out with other unemployed buddies at night. He hadn't even attended courses at a community college. The plan had been for him to enlist in the Air Force, but a weight restriction had delayed his enlistment. If he had spent a few months of those four years getting into shape, he would have been off into the wild blue yonder.

Well, the weight never came off; in fact, it increased. The heavier he got, the more discouraged he became. As his disappointment grew, he shifted the blame to his parents. Mom didn't cook the kind of healthy meals that he needed to eat. Dad wouldn't work out with him.

According to him, both parents only nagged and didn't understand how hard it was to get a job. Besides, did they want him to work, or did they want him to reach his dream? A job would hinder him from spending time at the gym getting in shape for the next Air Force physical.

This kid procrastinated about getting started on his exercise regimen, pouted when it was harder to drop the pounds than he expected, avoided confrontation by being out when his working parents got home in the evening, and was intentionally inefficient at finding part-time work. All of this was classic passive-aggressive behavior. And each day that went by with no change made his parents feel more helpless and guiltier about not drawing a line in the sand.

Another reason why boomerang kids feel entitlement emerges when both parents aren't sold on the idea of the child leaving. In more than one case I investigated, one spouse pointed the finger at the other, saying things such as, "His mother won't let me put him out" or "That's daddy's little girl, and he won't let her go." Kids are masters at playing parents against each other, and they've certainly perfected the craft by the time they're young adults and can see how to make things work in their favor.

»»» **PARENTAL PAUSE:** Attitude Check. Complete these statements and ask yourself these tough questions:

1. What are the reasons I place upon myself for why my boomerang child is home?
2. I carry a sense of guilt for my young adult's problems because I . . .
3. How is my child exhibiting passive-aggressive behavior concerning moving out? Is he or she
   a. procrastinating?
   b. pouting and sullen?
   c. stubborn?
   d. misplacing important materials (job applications, résumés, directions to the interview, etc.)?
   e. intentionally inefficient (seeming incapable of surviving on his or her own)?
   f. avoiding direct confrontation?
4. In what ways have I been buying into my child's passive-aggressive behavior, thus enabling him or her to remain home?
5. How have I been in disagreement with my spouse about our child leaving home?

## Respecting Boundaries

The Bible speaks of the preferred parenting technique for young adults who won't listen to their parents and exhibit passive-aggressive behavior. Deuteronomy 21:18-20 gives these instructions, in this case regarding a disobedient son:

> If someone has a stubborn and rebellious son who does not obey his father and mother and will not listen to them when they discipline him, his father and mother shall take hold of him and bring him to the elders at the gate of his town. They shall say to the elders, "This son of ours is stubborn and rebellious. He will not obey us. He is a glutton and a drunkard." (NIV)

That text goes on to demand the execution by stoning of such a child. No, I'm not recommending such an extreme response from parents today! But, the spirit behind this biblical passage is stern indeed. Boomerangs who refuse to listen to and obey their parents open themselves up to "dying" to their parents' kindness and handouts. And the parents ought not to be ashamed to bring in reinforcements from church leadership and respected family or friends when the adult child gets belligerent.

As I mentioned before, this boomerang phenomenon is not new, and it's also not confined to the United States. Several articles written a few years back still hold some remarkably good suggestions for setting rules that will allow you to relax, to weather the storms of having grown kids in your nest, and to experience the promise of Psalm 127:2d: to get some sleep.

Paul Majendie wrote an article for *Reuters Life!* in London, England, entitled "'Boomerang Kids' Driving Parents to Distraction." He shows that British parents suffer the same frustrations, and he ends with some practical rules recommended by an organization called Parentline Plus:

> Parentline Plus has been bombarded with desperate calls from beleaguered parents to their helpline. . . . Callers to the helpline are concerned about aggressive behavior—both verbal and physical—from their children and worried about their drug and drink consumption. . . .
>
> After researching the growing problem, the independent charity [Parentline Plus] suggested a set of rules to avoid domestic warfare breaking out on all fronts:
>
> - Get them to pay rent
> - Agree on household chores
> - Don't wait on them hand and foot
> - Speak to them if behavior upsets you
> - Be ready to say "I love you but not your behavior."[1]

After looking through quite a few articles about college graduates moving back home, I noticed that the guidelines for making it sanely and successfully through this season overlapped. A summary of the suggestions are as follows (in no particular order):

- Recognize that the person who returns is not exactly the same person who left home. Sure this is still your child, but he or she is an adult now and deserves to be treated like one, with grown-up expectations and responsibilities.

• Go into the arrangement with a plan. Discuss expectations and boundaries. The reason for your child's return should be clear to all concerned: to start a career, save money for a particular goal, take a break for a defined time period, prepare for graduate school, etc. Set clear expectations: Lay out your child's obligations regarding issues such as expenses, household chores, and having dates over for dinner. Write all of this down and revisit as necessary.

• Enter the arrangement with a supportive attitude. Determine not to nag. Explain that keeping the lines of communication open keeps the waters smooth. In other words, let your child know that his volunteering of regular updates about his job search helps you feel comfortable that he is keeping up his end of the bargain.

• Set a time limit. Go into the arrangement with an end clearly agreed upon.

• Discuss money. With the additional person in the house, all of the expenses increase. Lay out the reality of the additional electricity, gas, water, and food expenses. Charge rent or an amount that is understood to cover his or her portion of the amenities. Attaching a monthly financial commitment to the housing helps prepare your child for living independently.

• Be clear about each other's personal space and respect it.

• From the start, set up regular times to periodically check up on progress. At these meetings, both sides can express their opinions about how well the other side has kept its promises.

• If either you or your child recognizes a need for anything about the arrangement to change, sit down together and talk it over immediately. Remember, you are family and you love each other. Both you and your child want the best for each other.

## Getting Along without Parental Help

"I can do it myself." Parents begin hearing that assertion when our children are quite young. Kids want to tie their own shoes, choose their own clothes, and make their own lunch. I submit that we parents are the ones who thwart that inbred aspiration. (Remember the examples we saw in chapter 2.) But even now, we can start paving the way for the ultimate independence of our boomerang kids. Begin by changing your mind about how you see your kids: not as creatures dependent on you for life, but rather as ever-maturing human beings who are destined for independence. Provide opportunities for them to do things on their own and keep an eye out for signs of maturity. My friend Carmelita Lee told me her thoughts about this:

> I have always watched for signposts showing me that my teen or young adult was maturing. I watched for when they did something without being told to do it, or when they have tried to assist with something in my life that was before neglected by them. When you see this, it brings joy and tears to your eyes and spirit. This lets you know they are growing and allows for you to loosen up the strings and give positive praise. After you have given a three-year span of watching the child or children go from not caring to caring, this is the reward. Always remember that after you have given them responsibilities and tasks to be performed, give rewards and praise. Nothing fancy, but be cost effective. In the Bible there were rewards, and they were very simple but effective.

In my book *Raising Boys to Be Like Jesus*, I related a story about my nephew, Daniel Nelson. His story bears repeating here because it is a perfect example of the fact that kids are resilient, and young adults can figure out a way to get along without their parents' help.

> After graduation from high school, [Danny] was accepted to Ohio State University on federal aid with a plan to study zoology. Well, those college science courses were a little harder than he had expected, and he ended up unable to handle them. He lost his federal aid and his place in the program. His next move is what made me proud.
>
> Danny did not run home to his mommy. He found a job working at a campus-operated hotel. He rented a bachelor apartment and rode back and forth to work on his bicycle—yes, that's right, in Ohio, sometimes in the snow! He began to really like the hotel business and took up courses at Columbus State Community College to work his way back into the university. He successfully returned to Ohio State and graduated with a degree in hospitality management.

> Now my sister, Danny's mother, could have easily told him to come on home to California where he'd have a place to live, familiar surroundings, and family and friends for support. But she let Danny take the responsibility for himself as a young adult and work it out. Danny is now married with two children, a lovely home, and a career he loves in hotel management with a major hotel chain.[2]

I once asked the high school seniors I was teaching, "What is it you feel you need to know before you can comfortably call yourself an adult?" They had so many questions that they wanted answered that we actually outlined a book. My students suggested I entitle it *How Not to Look Stupid as an Adult*. It would have been divided into three sections: School/Career Stuff, Personal/Social Stuff, and Spiritual Stuff. For the School/Career section, they wanted to know things such as how to choose a good roommate, the best way to plan your college schedule of classes, and how to handle an unfair professor. In the Personal/Social section, they asked questions about filling out a rental application, establishing credit, and getting out of uncomfortable situations with associates. And they wanted to know a myriad of things about following God in this ungodly culture.

I've never gotten around to writing that book, but I mention it here because I wonder if you've ever asked your boomerang point-blank about his or her fears and concerns about living independently. As I was startled by some of my students' responses, you might be surprised by the insecurities that your child shares. You may think that your son knows things that in fact he's quite unsure about. Your daughter is likely to reveal self-doubts that you never suspected, which are the deep-seated reasons for her reluctance to fly the coop.

»»» **PARENTAL PAUSE:** Ask Questions. Find out where your boomerang's head is; in other words, open a conversation which has a goal of revealing your child's insecurities about leaving home.

1. What kind of lifestyle do you picture for yourself when you're living out on your own?

2. What, if anything, do you fear about living on your own?
3. What are your must-have's or your can't-live-withouts in regard to moving out?
4. If you have to live with a roommate in order to meet the financial obligations of rent, food, utilities, etc., what are your requirements for the kind of person with whom you can live comfortably?
5. If it were not possible for you to live here or if something happened to me (us), how would you survive?

Changing our view about our children may be difficult, but it's gratifying to think of them as responsible adults. Just our beginning to see them this way is apt to spur them toward more mature attitudes and actions. Then, even if they make mistakes, we can take that news without guilt, because we realize that adults take missteps from time to time. That's life. We archers will have developed an objective and unbiased way to view our adult children, and will then find that our bows are well-balanced and in the perfect position to continue to shoot our arrows toward their ultimate destiny.

"The LORD grants sleep to those he loves." Realize that the survival of your young adults is ultimately their responsibility, not yours. Good night!

**NOTES**

1. Paul Majendie, "'Boomerang Kids' Driving Parents to Distraction," *Reuters Life!*, February 7, 2008, http://mobile.reuters.com/article/lifestyleMolt/idUSSAT75557420080207 (accessed May 29, 2013).
2. Sharon Norris Elliott, *Raising Boys to Be Like Jesus* (Valley Forge, PA: Judson Press, 2009), 51.

CHAPTER 9

# Flying Arrows »»»

Like arrows in the hands
of a warrior are children
born in one's youth.

PSALM 127:4

Regardless of how many types and sizes of arrows that exist, all are designed for one purpose: to be shot toward a target. Arrows in the hand of a skilled archer will make it to the target at which they are aimed because the best archers are skilled shooters.

In the extended metaphor that I've used throughout this book, arrows are our children, and we, as parents, are the skilled archers using the bows of our instruction to guide them. During their young-adult years, the time has come for our arrows to be launched toward their appropriate targets. The arrowhead causes the well-shot arrow to stick; a bent or broken arrow forms a boomerang and so returns. The hard truth is that there will probably come a time when our home is just way too small emotionally for both us and our adult child. We'll have to face the decision to—shall I say it—kick the grown child out of the house. The best thing we can do for our young adults is to provide them the guidance they need, and then the freedom they need, to live independently.

Let's discuss pointing our kids in the direction of independence, pulling back the bow, and letting them fly.

## Time to Move Out

In preparation for writing this chapter, I asked folks to send me their thoughts on when they knew it was time to move out of their parent's house. The funniest response I received was from a pastor friend of mine, Vince Holmes. Here's what he said:

> I was about seven years old when I realized it was time to move out of my momma's house. I can't remember exactly what I wanted, but I remember her response vividly. She said, "As long as you live in my house, you are going to do what I tell you to do." So I put some clothes in a pillowcase, found a long stick, tied the pillowcase around the stick hobo-style, and planned to leave. Her reaction was, "Hold on. You're gonna need something to eat. Let me make you a lunch." I decided I could wait another ten to twelve years before I would actually leave.

Another one of the few responses that I received came from Barry Carson, a former student of mine: "I knew it was time to move out when we were arguing a lot. When I'm upset, I usually say, 'I'm ready to move.'"

Perhaps I didn't get many answers to my question because this is an area in which parents really have trouble. Maybe the problem is that we just don't know how to tell our grown kids that it's time to move—because our own parents didn't clearly articulate that message for us. Without that explicit example to follow, maybe we don't know what signs to look for to indicate that it's time for them to go. Or maybe, in some cases, we really aren't serious about letting them go.

## It's Time for Boomerangs to Leave When . . .

In order to learn how to operate our lives by God's standards, we can follow the examples that God left for us. From time to time, God's children got kicked out of the house for various reasons. Let's see why God ejected those kids, and I bet that we can apply these principles to our current situation.

### *They No Longer Respect House Rules*

Adam and Eve are our first candidates. Here were God's perfect creations, the very first humans. They must have been gorgeous:

the most handsome man and the most beautiful woman ever. God even took special time to craft for them a lovely living arrangement in the beautiful Garden of Eden. But they flubbed it.

> Now the LORD God had planted a garden in the east, in Eden; and there he put the man he had formed. The Lord God made all kinds of trees grow out of the ground—trees that were pleasing to the eye and good for food. In the middle of the garden were the tree of life and the tree of the knowledge of good and evil. A river watering the garden flowed from Eden; from there it was separated into four headwaters. (Genesis 2:8-10, NIV)

God planted the garden, offered abundant food supply to the man and woman who would live there, and even explained the garden rules very clearly: "You are free to eat from any tree in the garden; but you must not eat from the tree of the knowledge of good and evil, for when you eat from it you will certainly die" (Genesis 2:16-17, NIV). As long as the man and the woman obeyed the rules of the garden, they were free to enjoy its plentiful provision. But the moment they disrespected the rules, all that changed, and it was time for them to go.

That moment came all too soon, of course.

> Now the serpent was more crafty than any of the wild animals the LORD God had made. He said to the woman, "Did God really say, 'You must not eat from any tree in the garden'?"
>
> The woman said to the serpent, "We may eat fruit from the trees in the garden, but God did say, 'You must not eat fruit from the tree that is in the middle of the garden, and you must not touch it, or you will die.'"
>
> "You will not certainly die," the serpent said to the woman. "For God knows that when you eat from it your eyes will be opened, and you will be like God, knowing good and evil."
>
> When the woman saw that the fruit of the tree was good for food and pleasing to the eye, and also desirable for gaining wisdom, she took some and ate it. She also gave some to her husband, who was with her, and he ate it. (Genesis 3:1-6, NIV)

Why would Adam and Eve put themselves in such a predicament? Why would they jeopardize so much?

First, they were overwhelmed by an outsider. The wily, seductive serpent caused Eve to question God's clear directive. He subtly redirected her vision off of God's provision and onto God's restriction. There may have been dozens or even hundreds of trees in garden that God allowed her and Adam to use for food. By concentrating on the one restriction, the serpent spun God's positive into a negative. Instead of hearing, "Of every tree of the garden you may freely eat (except one)," she now heard, "You can't eat from every tree, can you?"

Second, it seems that they felt they had outgrown the rule. Eve looked at the forbidden tree and evaluated it for herself. It was pleasant to the eyes, good for food, and desirable because it could make her wise. She had outgrown her need for God's rule and replaced it with a new one of her own. In fact, she had three good, strong reasons to outweigh what she now considered to be God's weak one. She failed to realize that good looks don't mean good quality. Beautifully packaged poison will still kill you. And that's exactly what happened. (As a side note to women: that's a whole lesson on choosing men.)

Third, they were outdone by peer pressure. During the entire conversation with the serpent Adam was standing right there. The Scripture points that out definitively: "She also gave some to her husband, who was with her, and he ate it" (Genesis 3:6, NIV). The serpent beguiled Eve, but Adam participated in the sin along with his wife.

As with Adam and Eve, our young-adult live-in children can begin to see our rules as restrictive rather than protective. They figure that they've outgrown the need for what we have to say, and they want to do what they see others their age doing. When these attitudes occur, it's time for our young people to establish their own houses with their own rules.

### *They Are Entangled in Illegal Activity*

Our next candidate for his own apartment is Cain. Adam and Eve's firstborn son must have been their pride and joy. Then Abel, the second son, came along. How those first parents probably enjoyed watching their two rambunctious little boys grow up together! Once they became men, Cain and Abel went their separate ways only in terms of the jobs they did. Cain was a farmer, and Abel was a shepherd. Then tragedy struck.

> In the course of time Cain brought some of the fruits of the soil as an offering to the LORD. And Abel also brought an offering—fat portions from some of the firstborn of his flock. The Lord looked with favor on Abel and his offering, but on Cain and his offering he did not look with favor. So Cain was very angry, and his face was downcast. . . .
>
> Now Cain said to his brother Abel, "Let's go out to the field." While they were in the field, Cain attacked his brother Abel and killed him.
>
> Then the LORD said to Cain, "Where is your brother Abel?"
>
> "I don't know," he replied. "Am I my brother's keeper?"
>
> The LORD said, "What have you done? Listen! Your brother's blood cries out to me from the ground. Now you are under a curse and driven from the ground, which opened its mouth to receive your brother's blood from your hand. When you work the ground, it will no longer yield its crops for you. You will be a restless wanderer on the earth.". . .
>
> Then the LORD put a mark on Cain so that no one who found him would kill him. So Cain went out from the LORD's presence and lived in the land of Nod, east of Eden. (Genesis 4:3-16, NIV)

When our adult children are involved in unlawful activity, they must suffer the legal consequences of their actions. Notice that Adam and Eve were not consulted in God's punishment of Cain. They didn't argue in his defense; they didn't post bail. He was their son, but he was guilty. He had elevated his wrong to a new level, and God's judgment took over.

In our present-day lives, even if the move might be to the penitentiary, it's time for our grown kids to move from our homes when there's illegal activity in their lives. Adam and Eve remained Cain's parents, but they had to let him go into God's punishing hands. Although Cain suffered, he lived on, and God even protected his life. If our children must face such a situation, we too must allow the law to justly do its job, while maintaining a loving dialogue and a trusting faith in our God to protect them as they pass through the disciplining fires.

### *They Have Too Much Pride*

Next in line for a divine eviction notice is Nebuchadnezzar. The first three chapters of the book of Daniel tell about how God used the Babylonian king to punish the Israelites. But when God tries to get the heathen king's attention, Nebuchadnezzar just won't listen. By the time we get to Daniel 4, we see that Nebuchadnezzar's pride is so built up that he's ignoring all that he's seen of God. We take up the story in verse 30.

> [Nebuchadnezzar] said, "Is not this the great Babylon I have built as the royal residence, by my mighty power and for the glory of my majesty?"
>
> Even as the words were on his lips, a voice came from heaven, "This is what is decreed for you, King Nebuchadnezzar: Your royal authority has been taken from you. You will be driven away from people and will live with the wild animals; you will eat grass like the ox. Seven times will pass by for you until you acknowledge that the Most High is sovereign over all kingdoms on earth and gives them to anyone he wishes."
>
> Immediately what had been said about Nebuchadnezzar was fulfilled. He was driven away from people and ate grass like the ox. His body was drenched with the dew of heaven until his hair grew like the feathers of an eagle and his nails like the claws of a bird. (Daniel 4:30-33, NIV)

Nebuchadnezzar figured that he didn't need God, that he had gotten to where he was on his own. He actually forgot how God had been revealed many times before through Daniel and the other Hebrew boys, Shadrach, Meshach, and Abednego. Time and time again, the king had acknowledged the God of these Hebrews, but he had never come to the realization that it was the same God who was affording him all the greatness that he enjoyed.

One of my favorite scenes in all of theater is in *A Raisin in the Sun*, by Lorraine Hansberry. Beneatha, the college-age sister, decides to express her views on deity to her mother, on old-school African American woman who is an avid churchgoer and a staunch believer. When her mother replies, "God willing," to a comment that Beneatha has just made about her plan to become a doctor, Beneatha launches into this speech:

> Mama, you don't understand. It's all a matter of ideas. And God is just one idea I don't accept. It's not important. I am not going to be immoral or commit crimes because I don't believe in God. I don't even think about it. It's just that I get so tired of Him getting the credit for all the things the human race achieves through its own stubborn effort. There simply is no God! There is only Man, and it's he who makes miracles![1]

Mama slowly stands, walks over to Beneatha, looks her dead in her eyes, slaps her forcefully across the jaw, and pronounces, "Now—you say after me: 'In my mother's house, there is still God.'"[2]

Proverbs 16:18 says, "Pride goes before destruction, a haughty spirit before a fall" (NIV). Nebuchadnezzar learned that lesson the hard way, but learn it he did (see Daniel 4:34-37). When our grown children are consumed by pride, figuring that they have no need of God, they're headed for a fall. Unfortunately, God may have to get them by themselves and orchestrate for them a season of suffering before they realize how they should live. If we continue sheltering them in our cushy homes, we could be thwarting God's hand and silencing God's voice in their lives. Let the prideful boomerang go on out to make it on his or her own.

### *They Are Making Bad Choices*

In this category, we can include choosing to associate with unsavory friends, choosing to serve other gods (literal or figurative), and choosing to disrespect the God of your home. The children of Israel as a whole were guilty of all these things in the course of their history, and one bad choice seemed to lead to another.

After being warned repeatedly about steering clear of the heathen populations that they were actually supposed to destroy, the

Israelites struck alliances anyway. They began to intermarry and then worship the foreign gods. Bad idea.

It's the same kind of bad idea when our children begin to hang around with the wrong crowd. The apostle Paul warns, "Do not be misled: 'Bad company corrupts good character'" (1 Corinthians 15:33, NIV). It's even worse, though, when they deny God. Deuteronomy 29:25-28 makes it abundantly clear that God's anger is stirred when God's people worship other gods. That's what got the Hebrews kicked out of the promised land.

> And the answer will be: "It is because this people abandoned the covenant of the LORD, the God of their ancestors, the covenant he made with them when he brought them out of Egypt. They went off and worshiped other gods and bowed down to them, gods they did not know, gods he had not given them. Therefore the LORD's anger burned against this land, so that he brought on it all the curses written in this book. In furious anger and in great wrath the LORD uprooted them from their land and thrust them into another land, as it is now." (NIV)

When they decided that they no longer had any need of God, the Lord God expelled the chosen people from the land prepared for them. How dare they think that they could live in God's land, eat of God's produce, and recline in God's good weather, yet refuse to honor God as their benefactor? To the contrary, they wanted to earn from God's goodness and then spend it in worship to another deity. Absurd!

Well, it's just as crazy for our grown children to believe that they can subsist on the blessings that God pours into our homes, and then spend their energies (the energies that they gained by eating our food and comfortably sleeping in our beds) running with a raunchy crowd and glorifying a different god. The first commandment states, "You shall have no other gods before me" (Exodus 20:3, NIV); and when the devil tempted Jesus to serve him, Jesus reiterated to his adversary, "'Worship the LORD your God, and serve him only'" (Matthew 4:10, NIV).

It sounds harsh, but if we're to reflect God's attitude in all things, it behooves us to follow the Lord here as well. God has said of the chosen people, Israel, "You have forsaken me and served other gods, so I will no longer save you. Go and cry out to the gods you have chosen. Let them save you when you are in trouble!" (Judges 10:13-14, NIV). Kids bent on worshiping other gods should be made to do so in their own homes.

### *They Need to Embrace Their God-Given Purpose*

At the end of the moving-out line is Jonah. God didn't so much kick him out of somewhere as move him into somewhere. Jonah needed some special encouragement to fulfill the purpose that God had for him. He was not just sitting on his calling; he was avoiding it like the plague. Here's the abridged story taken from Jonah 1:1–3:3.

> The word of the LORD came to Jonah son of Amittai: "Go to the great city of Nineveh and preach against it, because its wickedness has come up before me."
>
> But Jonah ran away from the LORD . . . and sailed for Tarshish. . . .
>
> Then the LORD sent a great wind on the sea, and such a violent storm arose that the ship threatened to break up. . . .
>
> "Pick me up and throw me into the sea," [Jonah] replied, "and it will become calm. I know that it is my fault that this great storm has come upon you [the sailors].". . .
>
> Then they took Jonah and threw him overboard, and the raging sea grew calm. . . .
>
> Now the LORD provided a huge fish to swallow Jonah, and Jonah was in the belly of the fish three days and three nights.
>
> From inside the fish Jonah prayed to the LORD his God. . . .
>
> So the LORD spoke to the fish, and it vomited Jonah onto dry land.
>
> Then the word of the LORD came to Jonah a second time: "Go to the great city of Nineveh and proclaim to it the message I give you."
>
> Jonah obeyed the word of the LORD and went to Nineveh. (NIV)

Jonah was being stubborn because of his hatred of the people of Nineveh. From the full account, we learn that Jonah tells God that he didn't want to go preach to them in the first place because he knew that God would forgive them. In Jonah's heart, those people were so evil that they didn't deserve forgiveness, so he was going to be the last person to preach salvation to them.

Our children may be dodging God's call on their lives by remaining dependent on us. They may be humble, obedient, sweet kids, a complete joy to have at home. However, as with the little donkey on that first Palm Sunday, the Lord may have need of your child. It is up to us to loose them and let them go out on their own for the Master's use.

Contrast Jonah with another child of God in Scripture. Samuel was given to God at a very young age by his mother, Hannah. She had earnestly prayed to have a son, and once God blessed her with him, she immediately had the heart to give him back to God's care and service. We read this part of Hannah and Samuel's story in 1 Samuel 1:24-28:

> After he was weaned, she took the boy with her, young as he was, along with a three-year-old bull, an ephah of flour and a skin of wine, and brought him to the house of the Lord at Shiloh.
>
> When the bull had been sacrificed, they brought the boy to Eli, and she said to him, "Pardon me, my lord. As surely as you live, I am the woman who stood here beside you praying to the LORD. I prayed for this child, and the LORD has granted me what I asked of him. So now I give him to the LORD. For his whole life he will be given over to the LORD." And he worshiped the LORD there. (NIV)

Hannah knew from the start what we ought to know: our children are God's property, only on loan to us for a short time. If we are mindful of this, it will be much easier for us to launch them into their adult lives when the time comes.

»»» **PARENTAL PAUSE:** Have you noticed any of these signs indicating it's time for your boomerang to move out? Perform a reality check:

- Does your boomerang respect house rules?
  - Does your child feel that he or she has outgrown your rules, such as curfew, when guests need to leave, or keeping rooms clean?
  - Is your child overwhelmed by peer pressure? Does your child (and his or her guests) want to do things that make you uncomfortable?

- Is your boomerang entangled in illegal activity?
- Does your boomerang have too much pride?
- Is your boomerang connected with unsavory associates?
- Does your boomerang serve a different god?
- Does your boomerang disrespect the God of your home?
- Is your boomerang avoiding a launch into his or her God-given purpose?

If you answered yes to any of these questions, you may want to seriously consider giving your young adult a move-out date.

## Four Encouragements for Flying Arrows

As we launch our adult kids into adult lives, we must know the weight of the bow and line it up with the target if we plan to get the arrow to it. Grown kids must grow up. Here are four encouragements that we can give them as they launch. Encourage them to go up, slow up, pay up, and live up.

### *Go Up*

The phrase "take it to the next level" has worn out its appeal to me. My reason is that the phrase is predicated on the assumption that I'm not trying very hard. I believe that all of us ought to do the best we can do with the skills, talents, gifts, and information that we have at the time. If we are doing that, we're at the highest level we can reach.

I also believe, however, that when we find more light, we ought to walk in it. So instead of admonishing our young adults to "take it to the next level," I like to tell them to "take it to the excellent level." Don't just shoot for involvement; aim for significance.

Twin brothers Alex and Brett Harris wrote *Do Hard Things: A Teenage Rebellion against Low Expectations*.[3] These young men believe that their generation can make a difference in the world by choosing to do hard things for the glory of God. I believe that it's possible, and I highly recommend the book to every teenager, and especially to boomerang kids who haven't quite gotten the clue that they can make a difference on this planet. The five kinds of "hard" discussed in part two of the book can directly relate to launching out on one's own. Readers are challenged to move outside their comfort zone, go beyond what's expected or required, tackle what's too big for you to do alone, do things that don't pay off immediately, and go against the crowd.

### *Slow Up*

I am intrigued by slang terminology and love it when my teen students "hip" me to a new word or phrase. Slang tells a lot about a culture. The expression that fits here (which will probably be obsolete by the time this book goes to press) is "slow your roll." It means that you are trying or pushing too hard at something, especially something that you should have outgrown a long time ago.

Boomerang kids need to slow their roll on the childish things that they used to do. For example, a thirty-five-year-old boomerang shouldn't still be spending all his weekends at the club with twenty-two-year-olds. Slow your roll. At least some of those weekends would be better spent at business seminars. A twenty-seven-year-old boomerang ought to be making better use of her money than blowing it on turn-around trips to Las Vegas. Slow your roll. How about investing some of those dollars in an IRA and a home of your own? A thirty-year-old boomerang shouldn't be spending hours upon hours each day texting, connecting with Facebook® friends, tweeting, and playing video games. Slow your roll. Those hours would be much better spent searching for jobs, applying for jobs, and even taking classes at a community college to advance job skills.

Slow up. Let go of childish things.

### *Pay Up*

Healthy boomerangs ought to be working, relying on their own money, and living within their own means. Without my parents requesting it of me, I remember taking on some of my own financial responsibilities even while I was still in high school. I got a job after school at a community center teaching little kids to read. My goal was to pay for all my senior expenses myself. I bought my ring, my sweater, my t-shirt, my prom ticket, my Disneyland®

graduation night ticket, and my cap and gown. During my boomerang years after college, I covered all of my expenses: tithe; car loan, gas, upkeep, and insurance; telephone bill; personal care items; clothes; health insurance; student loan payments. By the time I got married and moved out of my parents' home, I was quite used to paying bills. The mortgage, utilities, food, and household items simply became new lines in my budget ledger.

Even in our current day and age, when men and women are supposedly equal, almost everyone I talked to about this subject felt more lenient about letting girls stay home longer than boys. Perhaps the violent nature of our times is a good reason for that. A young woman living alone may not feel safe. But let's face it: money (not safety) is the reason why most young adults are flocking home, so both daughters and sons need to learn the basics of money management. It takes money to live, so boomerangs need to be diligent about paying their own way.

### *Live Up*

That brings us to our final point: live up. Boomerangs must learn to live up to all of their obligations, not just the financial ones. A synonym for *adulthood* is *responsibility*. In addition to personal finances, an adult knows how to handle his or her responsibility in five areas: piety, personal character, punctuality, perseverance, and parenthood.

**Piety:** How is your child's relationship with God? Earlier in the book, I mentioned the alarming statistics concerning the number of young adults who have no further church involvement after high school. A responsible adult recognizes his or her need for the Savior.

Some churches seem to be doing a remarkable job with college-age kids. Like anyone else, your young people appreciate being around others close in age with similar interests. If your church doesn't have a vibrant young adult ministry, don't be afraid to allow your kids to join another congregation that does. The point is that they are serving God, hearing the word of God being taught, and growing in their faith.

Matthew, one of our sons, couldn't spend all of Easter evening with us one year because his church meets in the evening. At age twenty-three, he served as an usher there and needed to be at church early to get things set up for the service. He quickly ate dinner at home with us, but then he had to skip dessert in order to get to church on time. He attends weekly Bible studies and hangs out with the other Christians whom he's met at his job. Since he's living on his own, I don't see him much, but I'm in no competition with his church, not even on a holiday.

**Personal character:** Encourage your young adults to live up to the personal character that identifies them as upstanding human beings, stalwart members of society, and good Christians.

I spoke earlier in this book about our youngest son, Mark, and how he ended up securing a position as a manager for the university's girls' basketball team. What I didn't tell you was how his character paid off for him while in that position.

He had lots of fun traveling with the team when they went on their road trips to out-of-city and out-of-state games. From the sports budget, the coaches and managers received envelopes holding the money that they were allotted for meals. One time, Mark's envelope was a little fuller than usual. By listening to comments being made, he discovered that he had mistakenly been given one of the coach's portions. He gave the envelope back, exchanged it for his right amount, and thought no more about it.

But the coach thought about it. She was so appreciative of his honesty that upon return to the university, she took him into the financial aid office and rewarded him by removing his out-of-state fees for the following two years! In essence, he received about a 50 percent basketball scholarship, not for skill on the court, but for upstanding personal character.

**Punctuality:** Some famous people have said some interesting things about being on time. It was the Earl of Chesterfield who said, "Know the true value of time; snatch, seize, and enjoy every moment of it. No idleness, no delay, no procrastination; never put off till tomorrow what you can do today." Thomas Chandler Haliburton is credited with saying, "Punctuality is the soul of business." And George Bernard Shaw, always ready to turn a phrase, spun out this truth: "Better never than late."

Please encourage your young adult to respect time. Every one of us gets exactly the same amount of it every day. Young adults need to understand that when people use or reserve time for them, they ought to be grateful. Other time-sensitive considerations include getting to appointments on time by accounting for the traffic, the time it will take to park, and the time it will take to get from the car to the location. I tell my students: early is always acceptable; late is never an option. Being on time to work means that you are ready to start your actual job at the opening hour, that you are not just settling in. The person who is on time can be trusted and is in place to receive whatever blessings are being doled out.

**Perseverance:** The young-adult years can be tumultuous as your children try to find their place in the world. Assure your children that they can make it. You have poured good years and solid advice into their lives; they're ready. Let them know that there are no ups without downs, no peaks without valleys, no highs without lows. Don't give up.

You can effectively teach this to your children as they are growing up. Once commitments are made, stick it out. When we attended a small church of about seventy-five members, one of our boys decided to serve as an usher. The usher board consisted of several senior citizens and a few of middle-aged folks, but no middle-school kids. At first, he was really excited because he got a lot of attention as he stood in his aisle, doled out fans and bulletins, and passed the offering plate. Soon, though, the job got boring. The same thing happened every week, plus there were monthly meetings to attend on Saturday. When he decided to drop out, our answer was, "No. You made a commitment, now you have to stick with it." We agreed upon a six-month stint, and then he would have to choose another auxiliary in which to work. After his ushering days, he found his place with the recording and sound crew until he went away to college.

**Parenthood:** If your boomerang is also a parent, make it clear to him or her that your grandchildren are not your responsibility. You took care of your kids; now it's time for him or her to do the parenting work. If your boomerang is a lousy parent, get him or her enrolled in parenting classes. Enforce the rules of your house for everyone who lives there. If your daughter doesn't like your rules as they relate to the child, rental agencies exist that would be happy to rent her a space of her own. If your son is still thinking that he can run with "his boys" and leave his child with you, tell him, "Slow your roll. This is your child. Take your child with you." As a friend's mother used to tell her, "If you want to go someplace where you can't take your child, you have no business being there yourself."

»»» **PARENTAL PAUSE:** Plan out the encouragements with which you will bless your boomerang kid.

- In what ways will you challenge him or her to "go to the excellent level" and do hard things?
- How can you encourage your child to "slow your roll"?
- In what ways can you stimulate better financial responsibility in your adult child?
- How will you encourage your boomerang to develop piety, personal character, punctuality, perseverance, and, if applicable, better parenting skills?

Your arrows can fly!

**NOTES**

1. Lorraine Hansberry, *A Raisin in the Sun* (New York: Signet, 1995 [1959]), 76.
2. Ibid, 77.
3. Alex and Brett Harris, *Do Hard Things: A Teenage Rebellion against Low Expectations* (Colorado Springs, CO: Multnomah Books, 2008).

CHAPTER 10

# Aimed Arrows »»»

They will not be put to shame when they contend with their opponents in court.

PSALM 127:5b

An arrow can miss its target for many reasons. The problem might be with the arrow itself. Perhaps it's too light or too heavy. It could be made out of the wrong material, and it could be cut incorrectly. Or maybe it's not balanced. The problem might also be with the bow. Perhaps the bow is too large, too small, or too tightly or loosely strung. The problem also may be with the target. Maybe the target is moving, partially hidden from view, or just too far away.

And then, of course, there's the wind. Arrows fly through air. When the atmosphere is calm, the air doesn't have much of an effect on the arrow's flight. But, when the wind is turbulent, the arrow, the bow, and the archer may be fine, but the arrow's flight can still be disturbed.

Any of these scenarios are possible; however, the most plausible reason an arrow misses its target is found in a problem with the archer. You see, it's the archer's job to form the arrow correctly and choose the right type for the job. The archer is responsible for using the correct weight and type of bow. And it's the archer's judgment that determines if he or she is within range with a clear view of the target before letting that arrow fly.

In our analogy, all this speaks to the preparation involved in archery—and in parenting. As archer-parents, we have the privilege and responsibility of assessing the fiber of our children from a young age and seeking God's wisdom in shaping, sanding, and aiming our arrows in the direction we believe God is leading them. Of course, the analogy has its limitations, as we have seen. Children are not inanimate, non-sentient arrows, but human beings with free will to make their own choices, including their own mistakes. But with prayer and faithfulness in our task, we may trust that God will guide our well-aimed arrows in the world. "They will not be put to shame," and they'll even be able to confront with confidence those who oppose them (see Psalm 127:5b).

In their best-selling book *The Blessing*, Gary Smalley and John Trent teach us how orthodox Jewish families have continued the practice of passing a very special and biblical blessing on to their children. The family blessing includes meaningful touch, a spoken message, attaching high value, picturing a special future, and an active commitment. The underlying power of this blessing is that it supplies every child's felt need for acceptance.[1] I submit to you that, in addition to supplying our children with much-needed acceptance, we had also better give them some useable knowledge.

## Six Foundational Planks

Whether you are reading this book while your kids are young, or if you've been straightening out your boomerangs and forming them into arrows, it's time to build under them six foundational planks on which they can stand as you launch them out into their independent, adult lives. Keep in mind that children are most likely going to emulate what you demonstrate rather than what you elucidate. They'll do what you prove rather than what you preach; what you show rather than what you say; what you walk rather than what you talk. If you're not already doing so, start living these principles before your children so that they can see how the ideals work in real life. And don't be distraught if you have failed in some of these areas; we all have. Make some changes yourself as you teach. Knowledge is power. The truth is the light, and the truth does indeed set us free.

As I was writing this book, I sent out an e-mail, a tweet, and a Facebook® post that asked, "What's the most important lesson your parent(s) taught you that enabled you to live successfully as an independent adult?" I got some great responses from a few people that I have been able to use here as examples of the planks that I'm about to share. However, I was a little surprised that I wasn't overwhelmed by comebacks. I wondered, *Have parents had such an insignificant effect on their children that kids have absolutely no noteworthy lessons from their folks to share? Have our lives become so busy that we're leaving nothing poignant and positively memorable of ourselves to help our kids on their journey through life?* That would certainly be a sad state of affairs.

Each of the following planks is wide enough for you to decorate with your own embellishments. I invite you to elaborate on each, and at the end, using the basic types of planks, be the architect of your own foundation that you'll pass on to your kids. Just be sure that whatever you add is in line with God's word.

The six foundational planks to build under our children are the Spiritual Plank, the Behavioral Plank, the Social Plank, the Occupational Plank, the Financial Plank, and the Material Plank. These six planks are best laid by godly parents who will instill the biblical worldview about each area into their children.

### *The Spiritual Plank*

The very first plank to place in your child's foundation is the one pertaining directly and exclusively to God. In the film adaptation of Alex Haley's landmark book *Roots*, Omoro, Kunta Kinte's father, is shown taking his infant son out to a clearing, holding him up to the starry sky, and pronouncing, "Kunta Kinte, behold the only thing greater than yourself!"[2]

The very first thing that we should teach our children to be aware of is the reality, awesomeness, love, and majesty of God. Solomon put it simply in Ecclesiastes 12:13: "The end of the matter; all has been heard. Fear God, and keep his commandments; for that is the whole duty of everyone" (NRSV). My friends' parents laid this plank for them in various ways.

1. Put God first. Author and inspirational speaker James Watkins says, "I don't remember seeing *The Wizard of Oz* until I was in high school, because the classic film always aired on Sunday nights. And the Watkins family was always in church Sunday nights . . . and for Sunday school and morning worship and monthly carry-in dinners and youth meetings, and. . . . But more than simply church attendance, Dad put God first in daily life, in faithful financial giving, serving as lay leader, teaching Sunday school, being youth group sponsor, and serving others in hundreds of ways. Those priceless lessons have been passed down to my children and now to my grandchildren."[3]

2. Start each morning with a daily Bible reading. James also recalls, "When I would come downstairs to get ready for school, my Dad—before heading off to work at Kellogg's—would be sitting at the kitchen table reading his Bible. He never once said, 'James Norman, you need to read your Bible every day.' He just provided a consistent example of the importance of starting every day with a Bible reading—and so that's what you'll find me doing early every morning."[4]

3. God loves you and will never leave your side. My friend Lisa Copen emphasizes this truth and notes that it remains true even when you don't feel God's presence. "I was blessed to grow up in a Christian home where we were consistently assured that faith was not just a feeling but also a choice and that my sister nor I could never do anything that would make God, or my parents, love us any less. During lonely moments of unending pain, I have never doubted that God was still in control." Lisa's understanding of this truth has even helped her help us through her book *Beyond Casseroles: 505 Ways to Encourage a Chronically Ill Friend*.

4. Faith is personal. Another friend shared with me an incident that illustrates the point that faith is personal. When Karen Davis's mom drove her to college, her mom said to her, "I have carried you on my faith, now it's time to go on your own faith." This

piece of news frightened Karen at first. She was thinking, *Wait a minute. Does this mean I can't call home for money?* To her comfort, she discovered that her mom was talking mostly about the spiritual part of her life. (Backing off from money little by little would come later.)

5. Follow God's will for your life. My own son Matthew told me that he hears my voice telling him these words, encompassing one of the most important lessons of his life.

6. Have Heaven in view. I'll never forget hearing Dr. James Dobson's "Focus on the Family" program after he suffered a heart attack. As he lay in the hospital contemplating his mortality, he realized that the most important words that wanted to leave his kids were "Be there." In other words, in the face of death and the real possibility of opening his eyes in Heaven, Dr. Dobson wanted to be sure his children would be in Heaven too one day.

I totally agree with Dr. Dobson. Absolutely nothing can be more important in this life for us parents than to do our very best to guarantee that our kids get the message and confess Christ as Savior. In the end, the only thing that really matters is that all of us dwell eternally with God.

### *The Behavioral Plank*

Once the spiritual plank is in place, lay the behavioral plank. *Self-esteem* is a term that has been thrown around a lot over the years, but it is closely associated with the idea of acceptance that Gary Smalley and John Trent explained in *The Blessing*. And directly related to your children's positive self-esteem is their understanding of who they are to God. Your children are not only the apple of your eye; they're the apple of God's eye as well. Jesus came to die for them so that they could live, survive, and thrive.

The Behavioral Plank is laid to give our children the understanding that because they are God's, their behavior should reflect the Lord's image. Being like Jesus and listening to the Holy Spirit works its way out in the practical, everyday issues of our lives. We can start by teaching our children to obey the Ten Commandments. In Exodus 20:3-17 God commands,

> You shall have no other gods before me.
>
> You shall not make for yourself an idol, whether in the form of anything that is in heaven above, or that is on the earth beneath, or that is in the water under the earth. You shall not bow down to them or worship them. . . .
>
> You shall not make wrongful use of the name of the LORD your God, for the LORD will not acquit anyone who misuses his name.
>
> Remember the sabbath day, and keep it holy. . . .
>
> Honor your father and your mother. . . .
>
> You shall not murder.
>
> You shall not commit adultery.
>
> You shall not steal.
>
> You shall not bear false witness against your neighbor.
>
> You shall not covet . . . anything that belongs to your neighbor. (Exodus 20:3-17, NRSV)

My friends had almost as many behavioral lessons to teach as God had commandments, so they again gave me permission to pass these nuggets of parental wisdom along so that we can share them with our own children.

1. It's better to laugh than cry. James Watkins couldn't have developed his trademark sense of dry humor without the wonderful examples from his dad. His quiet, spontaneous wit continued to crack up the family even as dementia muddled his mind and cancer battered his body. Life tends to confront us with painful and troubling situations, but if we can take the edge off of those times with humor, we'll find the road through the hard times a bit smoother and a little less rocky.

2. You can fix anything with vise-grips, baling wire, and duct tape. James's dad was the "MacGyver" of home repairs! (In case you aren't aware, MacGyver was a mid-1980's TV secret agent who refused to carry a gun, and could troubleshoot complex problems using duct tape and a pocketknife.) I had to laugh, though, when I read James's account of fixing things because I had written an article years ago about what I learned from the fact that my own dad fixed everything with duct tape. The idea here is that young people ought to learn that things have value. Not everything has to be thrown away when it first breaks, and

we can transfer our knowledge of fixing things to our appreciation for bearing with the broken people in our lives.

3. Encourage creativity. James says that his family's garage was "a mad scientist's laboratory with every tool needed to create . . . go-carts, as well as marionettes, magical illusions, robots, and props for home-staged plays."[5] Our children learn patience by sitting down to create, and they should know how to do something with their hands. You never know when it may be necessary to earn some money using something that you have created.

4. Strive for excellence in everything you do. James remembers his dad as "a master craftsman, whether it was keeping the '56 Pontiac running, building a solid-oak desk that I'm writing on today, or keeping the garden weedless." From his dad he learned, "Anything worth doing was not only worth doing well, but doing with excellence."[6]

5. Never, ever say, "I'm bored." James quickly learned that if he dared utter the words "I'm bored," he would find a hoe, a rake, or a snow shovel in his idle hands. "And idle hands were the devil's workshop," he recalled, "so we were taught a strong work ethic. It served me well in school, work, and life."[7] It's a lesson that would benefit many boomerangs as well.

6. Don't be afraid of being alone. This is something that Barry Carson, one of my former students, learned from his mom. "The valuable lesson my mother taught me was to be a loner," he says. "I didn't want to accept that at first. Growing up, I was the only child and my mother was a single parent. I never got the worldly thing that made me popular. But as time went on, I eventually found out what she meant. She wanted me to be my own person in life." Our children should learn the art of being alone sometimes. They'll discover their own voice in solitude and be less likely to allow a crowd to drown them out.

7. Learn from failure. That's the lesson my son Mark says I taught him. "Failure helps me because I know what I need to do to improve, and it gives me a measuring stick for the future." This can be a particularly powerful lesson for our bent and broken arrows who have boomeranged home. Failures need not be a cause

for shame. They can become the means of self-improvement and a catalyst for change.

8. Surround yourself with good people. My son Matthew identified this as one of the most vital behavioral lessons that he learned from me. It is a good balance to Barry Carson's lesson about the value of being a loner. When our children do choose companions in life, whether as spouses or friends on the journey, learning to choose wisely will go a long way in advancing their personal growth—and possibly professional maturity as well. Consider the benefits for a boomerang who hangs out not with other boomerangs, but rather with friends who arrange to meet after their workday is over or on a lunch break. Such personal interactions may prove to be inspirational, motivational, and perhaps also rich in networking potential.

### *The Social Plank*

This foundational area contains the lessons that we teach our children pertaining to how they deal with other people. The Bible has much to say about how we ought to treat one another, but Jesus summed it up when he was asked to relate the greatest commandment. He said, "'You shall love the Lord your God with all your heart, and with all your soul, and with all your mind.' This is the greatest and first commandment. And the second is like it: 'You shall love your neighbor as yourself'" (Matthew 22:37-39, NRSV). Clearly, if we truly care about other people, there are innumerable ways to show such care that we can teach to our children. Here are just a few social lessons people shared that their parents had taught them.

1. Trust people until they give you a reason not to. Again, my son Mark shares that he learned this lesson from me. Having attended the small, Christian school where I was employed, Mark, and his older brother Matthew, had the experience of having me as their teacher in several of their high school classes. Mark recalls that part of my introductory lecture at the start of every school year always included the phrase, "I trust you until you give me a reason not to trust you." Mark has told me over the years that

this idea has helped him avoid pre-judging people. He has made some good friends because he has refused to think negatively about people before he has gotten to know them.

2. Presence is important. April Boyd-Noronha reflected, "The most important thing my mom taught me when I was a young adult is the simple principle of 'being there'. . . . As a single parent, she fully understood the importance of her presence. . . . Just to see her smile or the look of pride on her face was (and is) priceless."

3. Everyone puts his pants on one leg at a time. Lisa Copen shared this old Southern saying, noting that it "has helped me keep perspective when I felt like my limitations were holding me back from what God intended me to be. . . . I don't have to worry about what other people are accomplishing. Only I can have my testimony, living my life the way God intended."

4. Sand with the grain. This bit of wisdom comes from James Watkins's dad again. "Cut against the grain, but then sand *with* the grain to smooth things out." James points out, "Good advice for woodworking and working with people."[8]

5. There are no problem people, just people with problems. James Watkins says, "I'm not sure if that was original with my dad, but he certainly applied it. He had a big heart for 'people with problems' and befriended the friendless. Even the kid in high school who thought he was an alien—not non-American, but non-*earthly*—and invited him over to the house much to my utter humiliation. But Dad's philosophy has kept me in good stead with other people both personally and professionally."[9]

### *The Occupational Plank*

Some people live to work, and others work to live. The Occupational Plank offers our children steady footing through the advice that they get here concerning work and their career. We are mistaken if we think that work is a result of the curse given to Adam and Eve. Actually, work was part of human existence before the fall. It was part of God's good creation. Before sin, God had placed Adam in the garden of Eden "to tend and keep it" (NKJV). This happened in Genesis 2:15; the fall of humankind didn't occur until

Genesis 3. After the fall, the curse pronounced by God upon Adam said, "Cursed is the ground because of you; through painful toil you will eat food from it all the days of your life. It will produce thorns and thistles for you, and you will eat the plants of the field. By the sweat of your brow you will eat your food until you return to the ground, since from it you were taken; for dust you are and to dust you will return" (Genesis 3:17-19, NIV). Work itself was not a part of the curse; painfully hard work was.

Neither we nor our children should be trying to avoid work. We need to teach our children that the key to significant work is to do something that they love, something that they were cut out to do, something that God purposed for them to do. How do we know what that is? Start by helping them to discover their spiritual gifts. Several passages of Scripture outline the gifts for us. Study them together with your spouse and with your children, at various ages:

- 1 Corinthians 12:1-11
- 1 Corinthians 12:28
- Ephesians 4:11-12
- Romans 12:6-8

Once your children's spiritual gifts are identified, have them blend those gifts with their God-given natural talents and personality type. Bake it all together in the oven of prayer, and the meal that results will be their calling. For example, a young adult may have the spiritual gifts of knowledge, teaching, leadership, and wisdom. These gifts, coupled with a natural gift of gab and a sanguine personality, makes for an effective young-adult ministry leader or a company manager.

Some wisdom for this occupational plank comes again from my friends:

1. Put my work in the Lord's hands. Again, my son Mark shares that he has learned this lesson by watching us (his parents). He has seen how his dad worked for years at our city's power company, yes following safety rules, but ultimately trusting the Lord to keep him safe around all that high-voltage electricity.

Mark has also watched as I have trusted the leading of the Holy Spirit in regards to my writing and speaking ministry. God has repeatedly opened doors for publishing opportunities and speaking engagements. As Mark has moved into adulthood, he has had his own opportunities to place his work in the Lord's hands, and now he sees for himself how God moves in amazing ways when we trust Him with our livelihoods.

2. To plow a straight line—and life—focus on a fixed, far-distant point. Again, this is an important lesson that James Watkins learned from his dad. "That's good advice for life as well. Lock on to your dreams, goals, and intended destination; then don't take your eyes off of them for a second."[10]

3. You can change someone's life. Lisa Copen says, "Growing up, I constantly saw my parents reach out to people and encourage them. . . . [My] mom has become one who not only delivers food to those who are ill, but who actively uses ideas out of my own book *Beyond Casseroles: 505 Ways to Encourage a Chronically Ill Friend*. The giving to change others' lives has come full circle."

### *The Financial Plank*

Many people have a problem relating to money. They either hoard it or overspend it. All the hoarders think that they're right because they get a huge sense of comfort from looking at their money and carry about a fair amount of pride at what they have that others don't. They look down on the spenders as wasteful, short-sighted gluttons. The spenders think that they're right because they work to earn what they are enjoying. They feel disdain for the hoarders who vocally put them down all the time. The spenders see the hoarders as stingy and arrogant.

Including a solid financial plank of understandings about money will keep our children from many sorrows. It's true that we need money to live, and there's nothing wrong with it. While Scripture gives us guidelines about money, it only gives us an exact percentage concerning what part belongs to God—the tithe. What the hoarders and the spenders need to realize is that what we do with the rest, after we've given the tithe to God, is up to us as long as we stay within those guidelines. Get yourself a concordance, look up the words *money*, *riches*, *rich*, and *wealth*, and read verses and surrounding passages of Scripture indicated. You will have a more complete understanding of the mind of God on the subject. For our purposes here, there are a few key points about money that we don't want our children to miss.

First, God says that we're attempting the impossible if we try to serve both God and money. "No one can serve two masters. Either you will hate the one and love the other, or you will be devoted to the one and despise the other. You cannot serve both God and money" (Matthew 6:24, NIV). Both hoarders and spenders could be in sin when it comes to this verse. Hoarders are looking to their money as an idol, and overspenders are letting it rule their lives by needing to get more stuff or by being shackled by debt. God intends for all of us to have a balanced view and balanced usage of money. (*Money on Purpose: Finding a Faith-filled Balance* by Shayna Lear [Judson Press, 2012] provides a great overview of the four primary uses of money—spend, save, give, and invest—and how to balance one's natural tendencies with biblical and practical wisdom.)

Second, if we trust God with all our money, we'll be all right. We start with this trust by tithing. I taught my sons and my students that if they started tithing young, while they weren't making much money, they would form the habit of obedience and would not find it such a sacrifice later. The Bible states this clearly: "'Bring the whole tithe into the storehouse, that there may be food in my house. Test me in this,' says the LORD Almighty, 'and see if I will not throw open the floodgates of heaven and pour out so much blessing that there will not be room enough to store it'" (Malachi 3:10, NIV).

The best financial plan is to tithe, save, give, and then spend. So, we can start with our children by having four jars labeled as above. If your child receives ten dollars, one dollar (10 percent) goes into the tithe jar, one dollar goes into the save jar, and then the child can decide how much goes into the other two jars as long as something goes into both. Every Sunday, take the money in the tithe jar to church to place in the offering. The child can take the give jar money as well or can let that build until identifying a special recipient. Every other week or so, take the save jar to the bank and deposit that money into an account to be used only for long-term goals. Then help your child decide how he or she wants to use the money in the spend jar.

As we noted above, God promises to open the windows of heaven and pour out blessings for those who tithe and give. Not only that, God also promises to keep away those things that would devour our increase (Malachi 3:11).

Two people shared some additional monetary wisdom that was passed on to them on this financial plank.

1. Be honest with finances. That was an important lesson that Lynn Wallace, author of *Our Lifeship: A Study in Proverbs for Women*, learned from her dad. Her father never allowed bills to pile up. He believed the maxim "Owe no one anything" (Romans 13:8). "As soon as he received a bill," Lynn recalls, "he put it in an envelope with the invoice and sealed it. Then he handed it to Mom and said, 'Put this bill in the mailbox now.'"

2. Don't spend it just because you've got it. My husband, James, an exceptionally wise financial planner, always taught our kids this lesson, which he learned from his mother. His mom, Annie H. Benford, always had the money she needed because she was not a spendthrift. He, in turn, internalized that lesson and has been able to comfortably take care of all of our children's needs (and many of their wants) because he was careful with money, not spending it just because it was there.

### *The Material Plank*

If all the other planks are lined up properly, the Material Plank, the one that pertains to the obtaining and usage of "stuff," will fit in just fine. Our young people will be rightly related to God, have a healthy self-image, treat others right, work in the area of their strengths, and handle money properly. They will appreciate Scripture passages about blessings and be able to keep them in proper perspective. Amazing Scriptures will make sense to them, Scriptures such as these:

> Command those who are rich in this present world not to be arrogant nor to put their hope in wealth, which is so uncertain, but to put their hope in God, who richly provides us with everything for our enjoyment. Command them to do good, to be rich in good deeds, and to be generous and willing to share. In this way they will lay up treasure for themselves as a firm foundation for the coming age, so that they may take hold of the life that is truly life. (1 Timothy 6:17-19, NIV)
>
> Honor the LORD with your wealth, with the firstfruits of all your crops; then your barns will be filled to overflowing, and your vats will brim over with new wine. (Proverbs 3:9-10, NIV)
>
> So do not worry, saying, "What shall we eat?" or "What shall we drink?" or "What shall we wear?" For the pagans run after all these things, and your heavenly Father knows that you need them. But seek first his kingdom and his righteousness, and all these things will be given to you as well. (Matthew 6:31-33, NIV)

The only outside piece of wisdom that anyone gave me on this plank came from my husband, who taught the kids to enjoy a little of what they made. "Buy yourself a little something with every paycheck, even if it's just a pair of socks."

## Foundation Proclamation

How we handle each of these planks will add up to the legacy that we leave to our children, and how they handle them will equal the legacy that they'll leave to theirs.

»»» **PARENTAL PAUSE:** Now, using the basic types of planks, build the foundation that you'll pass on to your kids. You may want to type these out on a foundation blueprint. Read this to your child as he or she launches from your home, perhaps at the high school graduation party or on the night before the actual moving day to his or her new place. Customize one for each child, and print it out so that it can be framed. Following is an example drafted for my son Mark. Go to judsonpress.com and download a free PDF of a blank Foundation Proclamation to fill in for your child.

# FOUNDATION PROCLAMATION

***For Our Son, Mark***

We, your parents, love you and we are proud of you. The time has come for us to launch you forward into your adult life. You are a wonderfully crafted arrow that God has given us the pleasure of molding, shaping, and designing. Now is your season to begin your flight to your destiny. Here are some of the most important planks in your foundation on which we pray you will forever stand:

**Spiritual Plank**

- Keep Christ as your ultimate coach, director, paradigm, and GPS.
- Prayer is communication with God. Talk to Him, but also listen. As Pastor Pleasant always tells us, "When you open the Bible, God opens His mouth."
- Stay involved in a good, Bible-teaching, Bible-believing, Bible-following church.
- Memorize at least one Scripture every month.
- Love God and love your neighbor as yourself.

**Behavioral Plank**

- Strive for excellence. Always do your very best.
- Take care of your health. Get enough sleep, eat right, exercise, get regular check-ups, balance work and rest.
- Be kind.
- Smile. Laugh heartily. Cry when in pain (physical or emotional).
- Be thankful.
- Always remember that seasons—the good ones and the bad ones—change.

### Social Plank

- Be there for your family.
- Be who you are: let neither poverty nor plenty change you.
- Be a good friend.
- Don't pre-judge people; give them a chance to be what God made them to be.

### Occupational Plank

- Give an honest day's work for your pay.
- Keep getting an education; never stop learning.
- Don't step on people on your way up the corporate ladder.

### Financial Plank

- Tithe. Give God His off the top.
- Don't spend it just because you've got it.
- Save. That rainy day is coming. Live by the 10/10/80 rule: Tithe 10 percent, save 10 percent, live on 80 percent.
- If you hear of someone with a legitimate financial need that you can meet, do so and ask nothing in return. Treat him or her as you would want to be treated if you were in the same situation.

### Material Plank

- Believe God to help you to comfortably meet your needs (not your greeds).
- Do a little something for yourself with each paycheck.
- Take vacations.
- Once your needs are met, and all other financial obligations are handled, splurge from time to time.

## NOTES

1. Gary Smalley and John Trent, *The Blessing* (Nashville: Thomas Nelson, 1986).

2. Film adaption of Alex Haley, *Roots* (Garden City, NY: Doubleday, 1976).

3. James Watkins, "Top Ten Things My Dad Taught Me," *Hope & Humor—James Watkins*, http://www.jameswatkins.com/dadtopten.htm (accessed June 6, 2013).

4. Ibid.

5. Ibid.

6. Ibid.

7. Ibid.

8. Ibid.

9. Ibid.

10. Ibid.

CHAPTER 11

# Fletched Arrows »»»

Children are a heritage
from the LORD. . . .
Blessed is the one
whose quiver is full
of them.

PSALM 127:3a, 5b

One of the pleasures of my parenting was dressing my sons up for church and special occasions. I have a whole series of photos of Matthew and Mark, taken at different ages, standing back-to-back with their arms crossed. The portrait that started the tradition was taken in the outfits that they had chosen to wear for Easter. At five years old, Matthew was wearing white summer slacks, a mint-green, short-sleeved shirt, and a yellow tie, with a coordinated pastel-print sweater vest and cap. Mark was four and had picked navy blue walking shorts, a red shirt, and a white sweater with red and blue stripes. Classic. The boys took a picture in that pose again (not in the same outfits) in middle school, during high school, and at each one's college graduation. They have an appointment to pose again when each one gets married, and when each one has his first child. (By then, I'll come up with more important occasions to keep the tradition going until Jesus returns!)

These photos represent milestones and celebrations in our family. Now that these youngest two are grown and out on their own, these pictures remind us that the marking of special times as a family hasn't stopped. Their existence is still a reward, and we are happy to be the parents whom God chose to guide them into adulthood.

As arrows fly toward their target, part of what makes them so beautiful is their decoration. Fletched arrows are adorned with feathers, and the cresting of an arrow has to do with the application of color that identifies the arrow's manufacturer or owner. Similarly, parents do not become completely detached from our children when we launch them into their adult lives. The relationship simply takes on new dimensions. As I wrap up this book, I'll discuss celebrating our adult children's accomplishments as we continue to encourage them to make it out on their own. There are four basic ways we can continue to motivate and inspire our grown children.

### Energize Them

People are energized when they are celebrated. I notice that my students strive to do better when I celebrate their accomplishments. For example, I make a big production out of passing back research papers that have received "A" grades, and when students come through a difficult time and start picking their grades up, I reinforce the effort that I see with positive comments. The whole class gets involved when we give "props" (i.e., kudos or congratulations) to classmates who have accomplished something outstanding outside of class, such as shooting the winning shot, starring in the school play, or participating on a mission trip.

No matter how old our children are, we can and should continue to root for them. Ray Allen, a star NBA player, can look in the stands and see his mother, in her signature bejeweled jersey, rooting for him at every game. This man is grown with a wife and children, but his mom is still his biggest fan.

God continues to root for us, right? King David remarked, "I was young and now I am old, yet I have never seen the righteous forsaken or their children begging bread" (Psalm 37:25, NIV). He goes on in that same psalm to tell us, "For the LORD loves the just and will not forsake his faithful ones. Wrongdoers will be completely destroyed; the offspring of the wicked will perish" (Psalm

37:28, NIV). God reminds the prophet Isaiah, "So do not fear, for I am with you; do not be dismayed, for I am your God. I will strengthen you and help you; I will uphold you with my righteous right hand" (Isaiah 41:10, NIV). And the writer of the book of Hebrews tells us that God has said, "Never will I leave you; never will I forsake you" (Hebrews 13:5, NIV).

We can keep our grown kids energized by letting them know that we are rooting for them and celebrating who they have become. If they are attending a different church, visit sometimes. Continue to attend their special events. Attend their birthday parties. (Don't stay long. Just make an appearance, eat some of the food, and excuse yourself so that they can have fun with their friends.)

**Publicize Them**

We're great at being proud of our kids, so this suggestion is probably pretty easy for us to implement. Without being obnoxious stage moms or irritating bleacher dads, we can let others know what our kids are up to.

Matthew and I are each other's biggest promoters. While he was a student at our alma mater, Biola University, he suggested to his professors that I would be a good choice as a guest speaker for some of the context lectures in his program. It was my pleasure to speak with the college students several different times in this capacity. Those lectures and his continued suggestions garnered me a speaking time at chapel as well.

Reciprocally, I carry Matthew's business cards and keep my eyes and ears open to help him make the connections necessary for work in the film industry. Once, on an airplane, I was sitting two seats away from a gentleman who was reading a script. It would have been rude of me to lean over the woman in the middle seat to start a conversation with him, so I didn't make a connection during the flight. However, while standing in the aisle waiting to deplane, I ended up standing right beside him. I simply mentioned that I noticed he was reading a script, and that I had a son currently majoring in film in college. The man said that he loved to meet young people interested in the art, and he requested my son's information. I gave him Matthew's card.

Before I was even able to call Matthew to tell him about the connection, the man had contacted Matthew. It turns out that this man was actually the manager for an A-list celebrity! Matthew and the gentleman followed up with each other, and my son ended up working with the star on a local project.

God is not against publicity. Jesus told his disciples, "And this gospel of the kingdom will be preached in the whole world as a testimony to all nations, and then the end will come" (Matthew 24:14, NIV). And the apostle Paul explains,

> "Everyone who calls on the name of the Lord will be saved." How, then, can they call on the one they have not believed in? And how can they believe in the one of whom they have not heard? And how can they hear without someone preaching to them? And how can anyone preach unless they are sent? As it is written: "How beautiful are the feet of those who bring good news!" (Romans 10:13-15, NIV)

God the Father publicized the Son and was not embarrassed to tell us what the Son could do. "God made him who had no sin to be sin for us, so that in him we might become the righteousness of God" (2 Corinthians 5:21, NIV). Whatever skills your children have—especially if they possess competencies that can benefit others—publicize those gifts to others who may benefit by crossing paths with them.

### Harmonize with Them

God the Father's relationship with the Son and Jesus' relationship with the Father are perfect examples of the harmony that we can mirror with our grown children. Consider these verses:

- Matthew 11:27: "All things have been committed to me by my Father. No one knows the Son except the Father, and no one knows the Father except the Son and those to whom the Son chooses to reveal him" (NIV).
- John 3:35: "The Father loves the Son and has placed everything in his hands" (NIV).

- John 5:19: "Very truly I tell you, the Son can do nothing by himself; he can do only what he sees his Father doing, because whatever the Father does the Son also does" (NIV).

Of course, in the case of God the Father and Jesus (God the Son), Parent and Child are so close that it's impossible to tell them apart. Although their divine relationship can't be replicated in human relationships, their spirit of oneness can be reflected in our relationship with our grown children.

Examples of parents and grown children acting in harmony exist in some famous families. From the launch of their dream, well into their successful career, the singing group Destiny's Child was a family operation. The father of lead singer Beyoncé Knowles was the group's manager, and her mother was their fashion designer. Tennis champions Venus and Serena Williams rose to the top of their sport with their dad as their coach and manager. Tiger Woods took the golf world by storm under the guidance of his father.

God has given us wonderful biblical examples of family members working together as well. Let's look at three of them.

First, Jacob's relationship with his adult sons was contentious to say the least—plagued by the father's favoritism, the sons' jealousies, and then the older brothers' lies about Joseph's violent death (when really they had sold him into slavery). However, by the end of the Genesis narrative, much of that relationship seems to have been redeemed. The brothers were reconciled; Jacob was reunited with Joseph; and the entire clan relocated to Egypt when Joseph's rank and wealth could protect and provide for them. And upon Jacob's death:

> So Joseph went up to bury his father. With him went up all the servants of Pharaoh, the elders of his household, and all the elders of the land of Egypt, as well as all the household of Joseph, his brothers, and his father's household. . . . Thus his sons did for him as he had instructed them. They carried him to the land of Canaan and buried him in the cave of the field at Machpelah, the field near Mamre, which Abraham bought as a burial site from Ephron the Hittite. After he had buried his father, Joseph returned to Egypt with

> his brothers and all who had gone up with him to bury his father. (Genesis 50:7-8,12-14, NRSV)

Second, Esther lost her parents at a young age and was raised by a cousin, Mordecai. Even as an adult, living in the harem of a foreign king and made queen of the land, Esther obeyed the directions of her beloved guardian, despite the risk it meant to her own life. And in turn, Mordecai honored his adoptive daughter as a grown woman and royal queen by following her instructions.

> Mordecai told them to reply to Esther, "Do not think that in the king's palace you will escape any more than all the other Jews. For if you keep silence at such a time as this, relief and deliverance will rise for the Jews from another quarter, but you and your father's family will perish. Who knows? Perhaps you have come to royal dignity for just such a time as this." Then Esther said in reply to Mordecai, "Go, gather all the Jews to be found in Susa, and hold a fast on my behalf, and neither eat nor drink for three days, night or day. I and my maids will also fast as you do. After that I will go to the king, though it is against the law; and if I perish, I perish." Mordecai then went away and did everything as Esther had ordered him. (Esther 4:13-16, NRSV)

Third, Ruth chose to leave the home of her biological family and pledged herself to her mother-in-law, Naomi. The two women became devoted to each other, with Ruth working in the fields to provide food for their impoverished household, and with Naomi plotting to make provision for Ruth's (and her own) future.

> One day Ruth's mother-in-law Naomi said to her, "My daughter, I must find a home for you, where you will be well provided for. Now Boaz, with whose women you have worked, is a relative of ours. Tonight he will be winnowing barley on the threshing floor. Wash, put on perfume, and get dressed in your best clothes. Then go down to the threshing floor, but don't let him know you are there until he has finished eating and drinking. When he lies down, note the place where he is lying. Then go and uncover his feet and lie down. He will tell you what to do."
>
> "I will do whatever you say," Ruth answered. (Ruth 3:1-5, NIV)

Jacob, Mordecai, and Naomi knew the value of working with, directing, and teaching their grown children. And their children benefited from following the directions of their parents. Joseph's sons and his brothers became the twelve tribes of Israel; Esther's boldness saved the Jewish people; and Ruth became the great-grandmother of King David, in the ancestral line leading to Jesus the Savior.

No one knows our children better or has their best interests at heart more deeply than we do as their parents. Harmoniously working as part of your adult children's team is a beautiful way to keep continued encouragement flowing to them. That may take the form of becoming partners in a family business, or it may mean being the first number on speed dial when our children have a question about faith, health, finances, parenting, career, or automotive repair!

### Subsidize Them

Finally, it's not against any rules to build your children's confidence and boost them up by giving to them financially. I know you're probably saying, "I've been giving to them financially all my life. It's their time to make it on their own." That's true. And I'm not telling you to carry them. Remember, these are adult children you have taught, directed, aimed, and sent successfully flying out there on their own. These are not kids who are begging you for handouts all the time. When your children are productively making it on their own, financial gifts that help their business or lighten their load are tremendous blessings.

I'm all in favor of giving to charities and the needy, but why give all our excess income to outside organizations when we have hard-working young adults who could put that money to good use to help them get a little further along? If you have the means:

- Give them a prepaid gas card or a retail gift card, just because you're proud of them.
- Finance a week's worth of groceries when you know that an unexpected expense means that money is tight.

- Spring for an inexpensive used car when your child bags a fabulous, entry-level position at a stable company some distance from the home where his or her spouse is caring for their new baby. If an emergency arises, one car is no longer sufficient.
- Pay for six months of car insurance or for a two-year membership with a roadside assistance company.
- Pay two months of phone bills or student loan payments as a Christmas or birthday present.
- Purchase stock for them or a whole-life insurance policy for their young child.
- Underwrite the expense of the business license, logo, and trademark registration if you can see the promise of the great business idea.
- Buy your grandchildren's back-to-school clothes, occasionally or annually.

As you consider this area of blessing, remember these verses:

- Acts 20:35: "In everything I did, I showed you that by this kind of hard work we must help the weak, remembering the words the Lord Jesus himself said: 'It is more blessed to give than to receive'" (NIV).
- Luke 6:31: "Do to others as you would have them do to you" (NIV).
- Matthew 7:9-11: "Is there anyone among you who, if your child asks for bread, will give a stone? Or if the child asks for a fish, will give a snake? If you then, who are evil, know how to give good gifts to your children, how much more will your Father in heaven give good things to those who ask him!" (NRSV).

There are many, many ways to financially subsidize our adult children in order to encourage them to keep working hard. We're not spoiling them or going backward; we are simply reassuring them that we're behind them, that God's looking out for them, and that they're on the right track.

»»» **PARENTAL PAUSE:** Next to each heading below, write down one or two ideas that you can implement this month to fletch your arrows. Then revisit this list periodically with additional ideas you can put into action.

- Energize: In what ways can you celebrate the achievements of your adult children?
- Publicize: What can you do to get the word out about your grown children's gifts, talents, abilities, or business?
- Harmonize: Name some ways you can support or complement your child professionally or personally.
- Subsidize: If you were your adult children right now, what financial blessing would you need most? Plan to bless your child by meeting that need.